S0-CRO-882

4–6

TOGETHER WE CAN
IMPROVISE

Units based on stories and themes for teachers and teaching artists

LOIS KIPNIS ◆ KIM MCCORD ◆ LOUISE ROGERS

Alfred

Cover Design by Elaine Padilla • Art by Justin Surmani

© 2012 Alfred Music Publishing Co., Inc.

16320 Roscoe Blvd., Suite 100
P.O. Box 10003
Van Nuys, CA 91410-0003

All Rights Reserved. Printed in USA.

ISBN:0-7390-8013-X
ISBN-13: 978-0-7390-8013-9

CONTENTS

ACKNOWLEDGEMENTS

The authors wish to thank the following teachers who tested various pieces and activities: Jennifer Bland, Vivian Murray-Caputo, Leah Crews, Michele DeLong, Nancy Miller, Jennifer Rockwell, Debby Smith, Jane Thomley, Kara Vombrack, Rose Wright and Donna Zawatski. Thanks to Jennifer Bland and Gabe Myers for joining Kim on the recordings of the Orff instruments. Jennifer performs the recorder improvisations and Gabe and Kim perform the other improvised instrument solos. Many thanks as well to Eric Kalver for his elegant and tasteful work in syncing and recording key instrumental tracks. We appreciate the advice from Arts Technology Professor Aaron Paolucci and the excellent work of recording engineers Philippe Moore and Eric Fortin on the CD recording. Finally, thanks to the Office of Research in Arts Technology in the College of Fine Arts at Illinois State University for the use of their recording facilities and equipment.

TOGETHER WE CAN IMPROVISE

UNITS BASED ON STORIES AND THEMES FOR TEACHERS AND TEACHING ARTISTS

Together We Can Improvise has evolved from the authors' beliefs in the importance of developing improvisational skills at an early age, and the need for accessible lessons that include a variety of art forms and activities in order to ensure that students of diverse abilities and learning styles can actively participate. It is based on the authors' beliefs that music, movement, art, drama and classroom teachers can work together to provide experiences that will motivate students to read, write and learn.

A book on improvisation across the disciplines is needed more than ever now, in order to develop flexible, creative thinkers who are able to take risks, weigh alternatives, and solve problems. The more opportunities students have to improvise, the more they are able to listen to each other, empathize, and communicate expressively.

There are many books on how to teach musical improvisation, and others that focus on theatre and dance improvisation. What is unique about *Together We Can Improvise* is that each unit not only provides a variety of opportunities for students to improvise and compose as actors *and* musicians, but each unit is based on a story or classroom curriculum, thus enabling music, drama and classroom teachers to collaborate.

THE UNITS

A NOTE FROM THE AUTHORS ON HOW TO USE THE UNITS

Each unit is based on a story or theme, with ample opportunities for specialty teachers and classroom teachers to work collaboratively. We take teachers through complete lessons from Warm-Ups that utilize drama and music, to core activities, to follow up activities that enable the classroom teacher to extend the lesson. We have focused on our areas of expertise—drama and music, but art and dance teachers can connect, and use these units as springboards for activities in their classes.

Each unit is written so it can be used in part, or in its entirety. The music teacher, the drama teacher, or both can use it. The music and/or drama teacher can work in collaboration with the classroom teacher and/or artist in residence. Each unit provides an opportunity for a team to work together and provide a holistic learning experience for students. The myth "Pandora's Box," the folktale "It Could Always Be Worse," and Shakespeare's *Macbeth*, are brought to life through music and drama.

We have provided you, the teacher, with improvisational options that range from short exercises to complete scenes. Start at your comfort level. You do not have to do the entire unit (unless you'd like to) nor do you have to do each unit in the sequence we have provided. There are many ways to work with the units.

Our suggestions are as follows:

Preparation of Content

- Read the complete unit. As you read the unit, see what inspires you, and select those activities that you feel comfortable trying. Focus on activities that would further your music or drama goals, develop specific skills of your students, and would be appropriate for your class. We have indicated a grade level range for each unit, but you can adapt it for your needs.

- You can work on just one selected Warm-Up or scene in the Core Activities, or as many Warm-Ups and core activities as you want. There is no time-line established. One exercise can take one class period, or can be extended over several class periods. In the spirit of improvisation, there is enough material for several months!

- You can focus on only the drama activities, vocal or instrumental activities, or a combination of any of these. Start where you are comfortable and then maybe challenge yourself to try one drama activity if you have never done drama with students. Or, try one scat activity if you have never worked on scat with a class. These units can be a learning experience for you as well as the students. We find that the ability to improvise increases as one works in improvisation mode with students! One idea triggers another idea.

- Decide how you want to present each activity. We have provided specific directions to guide you. You can use these directions, or present it in your own style. In the Environment Unit, we have scripted dialogue to guide you through the exercises, but it is only a suggested dialogue. Use it as it is, or extract what you want from it. Modify! Improvise! Re-word! Have fun!

- Let the librarian and the classroom teacher know what you're working on. They may want to collaborate. We suggest that you time your work, if possible, to when the classroom teacher is studying something that is connected to one of the units.

- You will notice that when we give examples, we usually add, "etc." We want you and the class to come up with your own ideas, and improvise together.

★ These units are a great way to do creative student developed performances as an alternative to scripted plays.

If you teach at the university level and prepare teachers for the classroom, try some of these activities with them. Help them to think out of the box and feel comfortable with improvisation. If they do not *experience* improvisation, they may never feel comfortable trying it in the classroom. As the proverb advises, "Tell me, I will forget. Show me, I might remember. Involve me, and I understand."

Preparation of Students

Prior to working on these units, we suggest that you introduce students to *freeze* and *focus*, the concept of *special space*, and the *audience rule*.

Special Space

Explain to the students that many times they will be working at the same time and will need to work in a special space. This is a space where they can stand or sit, and put their arms out to the sides, in front of them, and behind them and no one is in their way. It is a special place for them to do their own creative thinking and improvising. Special space can be anywhere within the space you're working. It can be at their desks, chairs, or in a larger empty space.

Practice with your students. Have them find a special space quickly and quietly (you can do it in a special way if you like, such as: quiet as a mouse, or tiptoeing so you do not wake up someone, etc).

Freeze and *Focus*

Decide what you want to use as a signal to get the class' attention to have them *freeze* and *focus*. It can be the beat of a drum, or whatever works for you. Explain to the class that when they hear this signal, they are to *freeze*, which means to stop like a statue with no sound and with whatever expression is on their face or position their body is in. When they *freeze*, they also have to *focus* their eyes on you so they can concentrate on your next directions.

Practice *freeze* and *focus*.

- Have students find a special space. Have them shake their hands as quickly as they can, and then also shake their shoulders and elbows. Keep their hands, shoulders and elbows moving and move the neck, head, knees, and feet. Have them shake their body as fast as they can, and at some point use your *freeze* and *focus* signal and say, *freeze* and *focus*. Remind them that the signal means no sounds and eyes focused on you.

- Repeat the above exercise as wicked witches. Start with the wrists, then the elbows, shoulders, etc., until they have become the character. Use the *freeze* and *focus* signal.

Audience Rule

Explain to the class that many times they will be the audience, the ones who watch and listen to the actors and musicians. When they're in the audience, their job is to sit quietly and to focus on the actors and musicians. The audience cannot call out ideas for the improvisers/performers (unless they're asked to). They cannot improvise/perform while sitting in the audience (unless they're asked to). Tell them that if they hear you say "audience rule," that means that someone has forgotten to be an attentive member of the audience.

Your Role Throughout Each Activity

Everyone has a different style and method for guiding students through drama and music activities and encouraging creative thinking. Since our main goal is to have students acquire the ability to improvise, think on their feet, and think of creative solutions and creative ideas, we suggest that as you guide the students through the exercises, ask questions that challenge them to add details and to think of new ideas. For example, if they're pantomiming eating a slice of pizza, side coach from wherever you are in the room with, "What else do you do when you eat pizza? What happens if it is too hot when you take a bite, or too peppery? How do you hold a slice of pizza?," etc. If they're in a conflict argument and trying to convince someone to do something or see their point of view, side coach with, "What are some other solutions to the problem? Can you add reasons? Can you work out a compromise?," etc.

Basic Instruments

Hand drums and rhythm sticks are very affordable and can be found at various music stores and online resources. Rhythm sticks can be made from wooden dowels. To get the most variety of sound, purchase rhythm sticks with ridges on them. We recommend small and medium sized drums that are actual drums rather than the flat, geometric shaped drums. Egg shakers are easy for children to handle and one or two triangles are great for producing metal sounds. Wood blocks, finger cymbals, a tambourine, a ko-ko-rico and other color instruments are wonderful. In music classrooms Orff instruments enable accompaniments to be realized. Boomwhackers can be used in some of these pieces, but generally they won't work for improvised solos or very complex accompaniments.

WARM-UPS TO INTRODUCE IMPROVISATION TO STUDENTS

DRAMA

If your class is unfamiliar with pantomime, conflict improvisations, and role-playing, you might want to engage them in some simple exercises before you begin work on the units. You can use your own exercises or the following:

Pantomime

Explain that pantomime is when you act without words, sounds or real objects.

- Have everyone find a special space and imagine they're entering their school's annual bubble-gum blowing contest. There's a trophy for the person who can blow the biggest bubble (it cannot pop). Tell them you're one of the judges, and while you and the other imaginary judges are preparing the score sheets, they should take an imaginary piece of gum out of its wrapper, put it in their mouths, and chew it so it is ready for a good bubble! Tell them to focus on details. How do they unwrap the gum? How do they chew it? Guide them through the contest: "Okay. The judges are ready. On your mark, get set, go. Blow that bubble. Focus on the bubble. See it getting bigger and bigger and bigger. You really want that trophy. Concentrate. Oh no, the bubble just popped. (Remind them no sounds!) It's all over your face. How do you get gum off your face? How do you feel? Use your faces and bodies, but no words. *Freeze.* What if you won the contest? Let me see how you feel (without sounds). Pose with your trophy so I can take a picture of you. *Freeze."*

- Explain that in many of the activities, they will be using their five senses as they pantomime. Review the five senses, and have them pantomime the following: *See* a funny movie (no sounds!); *hear* a scary sound; *smell* a skunk; *taste* their favorite candy; *touch* glue. Remind them with each one to use their faces and bodies to express how they feel, and to *really* see or hear, etc.

Role-playing/Characterization/Conflict Improvisation

In each unit, students will become different characters with different emotions in different situations. Many of these situations will involve conflict (two or more people want something different, or a person has an inner conflict or a conflict with the environment). To introduce the idea of role-playing and conflict, have the class sit in a special space. Explain, "I am going to role-play (play the character) a parent, and you are all going to role-play (play the character) the child. Pretend that your friend's dog just had puppies, and he or she wants to give you one at no cost. You have always wanted a puppy. Your parent has always said, *No puppy!"*

"Let's imagine you just approached your parent, and your parent has once again said *no!* One at a time, I want each of you to say something or do something that will convince me to let you have the puppy. The challenge is that once a person had said something or tried a certain approach, it cannot be repeated. You have to persuade me. You have to convince me that you should have this puppy.

Think of reasons why it would be good to have a puppy (get exercise, protect against robbers, etc.) Work out solutions. Listen to each other."

Begin the improvisation with one student asking you for the dog; and your response. Then, have one student at a time try to convince you; you will also have to improvise and think of responses to each one. What would you say if the child says to you that he or she promises to walk the dog, or will earn money, etc.? Might you answer back with, "You won't even walk your younger sister to her friend's house when it is cold outside; why should I believe you will walk the dog?" Each rebuttal from you will challenge students to think and respond with new ideas and solutions (the goal of improvisation).

At some point when you think all reasons and possible solutions have been exhausted, try to make deals or compromises, or end the improvisation. Then, explain to the class that what they just did was role-play and improvise. They did not read from a script or write what they would say. They did not plan what they would do or say. They listened to each other and created dialogue and actions "on the spot." This is what we call improvisation.

VOCAL

Throughout this book, we will explore the voice and all that it has to offer. Teachers and students will be asked to use their voices in unique ways. There are many ways to improvise vocally. At times you will be asked to make silly sounds, loud sounds, mechanical sounds, animal sounds; big, little and scratchy sounds; mysterious, coaxing, persuasive, dissuasive, scary and peaceful sounds, among many others.

The idea that vocal improvisation means singing anything you want is not quite true, and often is not very helpful. The vocal activities provided in the book are meant to guide you and give you structure as you improvise.

We create these sounds and are always mindful of the fact that we never want to mistreat the voice. As teachers we need to model good vocal technique. Always give a starting pitch when singing as a group and lead the class in singing on pitch. Never allow the students to sing too loudly. This could damage the voice. Loud sounds such as car alarms should be sung with plenty of head voice. The vocal exercises in this book are meant to open the voice and strengthen it. If you feel that the class is singing incorrectly, stop them and model the correct way to produce the sound.

Body Percussion

Arrange the class in a circle and have everyone tap a steady beat (clap, pat, or snap, etc.) As the class continues the steady beat, students will take turns creating new patterns. These new patterns can be created by using body percussion: putting the rhythmic pattern in different places of the body. For example: head, chest, knees, hands, mouth, feet, fingers, lips, tongue, etc.

Dynamics

Boop Boop Pattern

Slides and Dynamics

Syncopation

Arrange the class in a circle and have everyone sing a middle C on "Hoo" (a quarter note pattern works well). As the class continues singing "Hoo" with a steady beat, students will take turns exploring loud and soft as they vocally zig zag and slide. Introduce the element of surprise and demonstrate the dynamic range of the voice. Once they get the hang of this, you can try putting dynamics on a pattern.

Scat

Scat Phrases

Scat Phrases Connected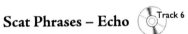

Scat Phrases – Echo

Scat is the jazz language of singers. Vocalists make up nonsense words while trying to make their voices sound like instruments. Practice these scat phrases with the class by having them echo you. Whether or not they are sung or spoken, be expressive with your voice.
- Buh-doo-Bah
- Beedle-ee-Bop!
- Za-buh, Za-Doo!
- Wheeeeeeeeeeee-Bop!
- Feedle-dee-Deedle-dee Dop!

INSTRUMENTAL

Improvisation in music is creating satisfying sound. If the sound is satisfying to the student then the improvisation is successful. It is a good idea to regularly ask the students if their improvisations sounded the way they expected them to and why or why not. If the students can articulate the answer to this question, they are closer to understanding what makes a good improvisation. It helps the other students hear their peers talk about their solos and helps everyone to understand how to think about sound and music. Encourage the students to discuss improvisation. Sometimes when children explain abstract concepts to each other, they can explain better than adults.

Found Sounds

Found sounds can be anything that makes an interesting sound that isn't an instrument. For example, how many ways can you create different sounds with a single sheet of paper? A paper can be torn, wrinkled, blown on the edge, rubbed, etc. What would a key sound like scraped across the edge of a metal trashcan? Found sounds can also be items brought in from home that the students share.

Improvisation on Orff Instruments- set up in a Pentatonic Scale

Limiting students to a few notes on Orff instruments helps them to feel less overwhelmed when you ask them to improvise on barred instruments. Many of the pieces in this book are written in a pentatonic scale. Improvisation can be performed using the pentatonic scale. Remove the bars not used.

Find ways to play hand drums, rhythm sticks, triangles, shakers, tambourines and other common instruments in non-traditional ways

Discover other ways to produce satisfying sounds on the instruments. For example, how many ways can you play a triangle? What happens if you make a circle inside the triangle and strike all the edges of the triangle? Do all corners of the triangle sound the same? What if you play it with a paper clip? A pencil? An eraser? Improvisers like to find ways to produce original sounds on their instruments.

Set some guidelines of how to play hand drums without damaging them

Most hand drums should not be played with hard sticks, and some are also too fragile to withstand using even mallets on them (thus the name hand drum). Using softer materials will work. Avoid anything wet or heavy, as well.

PANDORA'S BOX

Objectives

- Students will be able to express story themes and characterization through improvisation in music and drama
- Students will know the structure and elements of a myth
- Students will collaborate and select characters, settings, and best ways to dramatize a scene
- Students will develop improvisations into scenes for shared performances
- Students will demonstrate an understanding of the characters they portray by creating appropriate dialogue and using appropriate voices, body movement and gestures
- Students will collaborate to establish playing spaces for their dramatizations, select props, and utilize the space for staging
- Students will work to express the themes, plot, characters and settings through music (instrumental and vocal) and drama and see how each art form enhances a scene
- Student will evaluate their improvisations and try alternate ways to develop each scene
- Students will perform expressively on instruments
- Students will sing expressively
- Students will develop arrangements of pieces they learn to play or sing

National Standards for Theatre: Standard #1, 2, 3, 4, 6, 7
National Standards for Music: Standard #1, 2, 3, 4, 6, 7, 8, 9

Materials

- Collections of Greek Myths
- Boomwhackers, hand drums, recorders, soprano, alto, bass metallophones, soprano, alto, bass xylophones, contra bass bars, soprano and alto glockenspiels, triangle, chime tree. Some of these instruments can be substituted with boomwhackers or pieces can be performed without Orff instruments (see specific pieces for ideas)
- Scarves, pieces of fabric
- Pronunciation guide for character's names can be obtained online

Prior Knowledge

- Students are familiar with the definition of improvisation in music and drama
- Students are familiar with the definition of a myth
- Students are familiar with the definition of pantomime
- Students are familiar with the pronunciations of the characters in the myth
- Students know how to play various unpitched percussion instruments
- Students know how to play Orff instruments

INTRODUCTION TO THE UNIT

NEEDS INTRODUCTION TO THE UNIT TO BE CONSISTENT WITH K-3 BOOK!

IMPROVISATIONAL WARM-UPS

WARM-UP #1

- Review *special space*, *freeze and focus*, *audience rule*, *role-playing*, and *pantomime*.

- Ask students if they have ever received a present and been told not to open it until a later time, but wanted to peek. Have they ever been told not to do or touch something, and been tempted to do it? Explain that they're going to explore a story that includes serious consequences as a result of a curious person's actions.

- Ask students to imagine that a box decorated with masks and serpents has been delivered to their house. They did not see the messenger who delivered it, but they heard an evil and terrifying voice that warned them: "Never open the box, or evil things will happen."

DRAMA

- Have students select a partner and find a special space with their partner. One person in each pair is curious and wants to open the box in spite of the warning, and the other person does not want to open the box. At a signal from you, everyone will improvise simultaneously **without words**. Challenge them to use only facial expressions and gestures, and to imagine the box is within their space. Signal them to begin, allow time to improvise, and give the *freeze* signal to conclude.

- Now focus on one pair at a time. Explain that this time when you point to each pair, they must persuade and convince each other. They can't yell or argue. Challenge them to think of a variety of reasons *why* the box should or should not be opened, and different *ways* to convince the other person (plead, scare, make deals, bribe, etc.). Have them think about what they do and say in real life when they want someone to do something, and the other person refuses. What do they think is in the box that makes them want to open or not open the box? Who was the messenger? Why do they think he gave them the warning? Should they believe him? *Explain that they are* **NOT to open the box.** Later, when they improvise a story about this box, the box will be opened. As you point to each pair (one pair at a time), they begin the improvisation.

- **Note:** During each improvisation you can warn them in an ominous voice, "Do not open the box or evil will happen," or coax them in a pleasant, tempting voice, "Please open it."

★ To keep the class engaged while each pair takes its turn, ask the class to note the variety of persuasive techniques used in each improvisation, and discuss these with the class at the completion of the exercise.

VOCAL

Below are some ideas to get you and the students started with vocal exploration. **Always demonstrate proper vocal technique and do not allow students to mistreat their voices by singing too loudly.**

+ Lead the class in call and response, or select students to be the leaders and explore all of the listed vocal sounds below.

+ Discuss how to make the sounds evil, ominous, luring, beautiful or peaceful.

+ Which high or low sounds would persuade or dissuade them from opening the box?

★ Remind the students that all of these sounds can be adjusted with dynamics. Some sounds, like a baby owl, may be naturally soft. However, even a baby owl can get upset and have many different qualities to the "HOO." A mama owl may be naturally mature sounding, but can still sound mad, happy, loud and sad. Many of the sounds can be high and low. For example, a siren or elephants' sounds can go from high to low or low to high.

High Vocal Sounds: (high refers to pitch not dynamics)

How high can your voice go? Instruct the students to be:

+ a siren (fire engine, police car, an English siren)
+ a car alarm
+ a car screeching to a stop
+ a squeaky door
+ an angel singing
+ scared
+ yawning
+ a dog whimpering
+ a dog yapping
+ a dog singing "Row, Row, Row Your Boat"
+ a wolf howling
+ a cat meowing
+ a mosquito buzzing
+ a ghost
+ an evil sound (high)

- a witch's laugh
- an opera singer singing a high note
- a train whistle
- a bird (hawk, seagull, loon, mourning dove, etc.)
- a trumpet
- a flute
- Ask the students for other high sounds

Low Vocal Sounds: (low refers to pitch not dynamics)

How low can your voice go? Instruct the students to be:

- a race car engine shifting through the gears
- a ghost
- a dog growling
- a grizzly bear
- a fog horn
- a contrabass (an acoustic bass or string bass)
- a tuba
- thunder
- a yoga chant
- an elephant
- a lion or a tiger
- a fly or bumblebee buzzing
- an evil laugh
- the giant from Jack and the Beanstalk (Fee Fie Foh Fum)
- yawning
- Ask the students for other low sounds

Simple Body/Vocal Percussion:

Let's now think about how we can use the body as an instrument and how the voice and body could create sounds to persuade or dissuade us from opening the box. Lead the class in call and response or select students to be the leader. How low can your voice go? Instruct the students to try various sounds:

- clapping
- tapping knees
- tapping chest
- tapping feet
- stomping feet
- swishing hands
- snapping
- whistle and sing at the same time (flying saucer sound)
- smacking lips together to create a percussive pop/smack with the lips
- smack lips together to make the kissing sound
- tongue click

- motor mouth (lips together to make a motor sound)
- tongue trill (tongue on the roof of the mouth similar to a rolled "R" - keep the sound going, adding vocal sound or just the sound of the tongue trill)
- gently tapping the mouth while singing "ah" or any vowel
- snoring, snorts
- finger flicks
- one handed clap (fingers hit against palm of hand to make a muted clapping sound)
- finger rubs (rub fingers against thumb of same hand—when many people do this at the same time, it can sound like rain)
- wind
- Ask students what other sounds they can make with their bodies or mouth.

Note: Students can transfer the sounds to instruments.

★ Keith Terry is a drummer who has turned body percussion into an art. Videos are posted on YouTube and on the Keith Terry website.

Make a chorus of improvisational sounds

Explain to the students that throughout the story there will be opportunities for them to be a choir of sounds.

- Divide students into three groups: high sounds, low sounds, body/vocal percussion.

- Direct students as if you're directing a choir—using dynamics and steady tempo (this piece is completely improvised).

- Ask for soloists.

- Switch so that everyone has a chance to be each of the different voices. A student could also conduct this fun activity.

- Create a choir of sounds that persuades someone to open the box. Then create a choir that dissuades someone from opening the box. Then create a double choir that speaks/sings alternately. One choir tries to persuade and one choir tries to dissuade. This can be a lot of fun as the choirs talk and sing to each other!

INSTRUMENTAL

- Engage the class in a discussion about what instruments, found objects, or sounds are appealing and suggest that something good is contained in the box. What instruments, found objects, or sounds would lure them to open the box?

- Engage the class in a discussion about what instruments, found objects, or sounds are ominous and cautionary, and suggest something evil is in the box. What instruments, found objects, or sounds would convince them to leave the box alone and not open it?

- Play or have students improvise music that suggests evil. After the completion of the activity, ask students if they think the sounds represent evil? How? Do they have any other ideas? Would they open a box that contained those sounds?

- Play or have students improvise music that suggests peace and hope. After the completion of this activity, ask the students if they think the music sounds like peace and hope. Do they have any other ideas? Would they open a box that contained those sounds?

- Play both sounds simultaneously, and ask the students if they think the music is complementing the mood they want to show. Would they open a box that contained both sounds?

- This can be done as a teacher led activity or a student "hands on" exploration of various instruments and found sounds.

- Students take turns standing next to the imaginary box, listen to the music, and observe whether they move toward or away from the box.

- Try to avoid making any judgments about correct answers. Let students choose whatever instrument they want and then explore why they chose that particular instrument. Ask them what do they hear in the sound of the music that describes hope or fear. Ask them if they think the instruments convey that mood, the voices, or a combination of these, and why.

CORE ACTIVITIES

- Explain to the class that they will now improvise, scene by scene, "Pandora's Box," a Greek myth about how evil came into this world. **Note:** There are many versions of this myth, but this is our version.

- Review or define *myth*.

★ It is helpful if this unit is done in conjunction with the classroom study of mythology so that the classroom teacher or librarian can help students gather information on the gods and goddesses.

SCENE ONE

Explain that in the first scene, powerful Zeus, ruler of the world, looks down from Mt. Olympus, where the gods and goddesses live, and decides that Earth is boring. There are no animals or people. He calls Epimetheus, another god, to go down to Earth and create animals and to give each one a special gift for protection.

DRAMA

+ Have the class generate a list of animals (real or imagined) that Epimetheus can create, and what gifts he will give them (turtle/shell; porcupine/quills; lion/roar; skunk/odor; a kangahorse/ hopping, good kick, etc.).

+ Select someone to role-play Epimetheus, and about 8-10 students to be the animals. Have each student portraying an animal sit in a special space, and tell the class which animal they will portray (each one must be a different animal).

+ Instruct Epimetheus to improvise dialogue as he creates each animal (one at a time works best!) and gives it its gift of protection. Challenge him to improvise different ways to create the animals. Does he create them from trees? From rocks? With a swoosh of the hands? With words? With music? With vocal sounds? Elicit other ideas from the class.

+ As Epimetheus creates each animal and brings each one to life, allow time for the animal to act, and then return to its special space.

+ *This scene can be repeated with another student role-playing Epimetheus, and other students as different animals.*

VOCAL AND INSTRUMENTAL Track 7

Vocal and instrumental come together for this scene as the animals display their gifts. This is a challenging piece with a great groove that should be fun for everyone involved.

+ Familiarize students with "The Animals' Gifts" (**CD Track 7**) on the accompanying CD. The written music can be found on page 20. Explain to the students that they will learn the instrumental parts of this piece. The students will also be adding instrumental and vocal improvisations.

+ You may have the students sing and play "The Animals' Gifts" or use the accompanying CD, letting the students improvise with the recorded music.

Preparing the students for Vocal and Instrumental Improvisations

+ Encourage students to explore animal sounds. The students can sound like animals with their voices or with the instruments. Not everyone will be able to have a solo. Ask for volunteers.

+ Teach the students the piece, "The Animals' Gifts." Follow the written instructions, and add the vocal and instrumental improvisations at the correct time.

Teaching Process

- Teach alto xylophone part by rote and layer both parts together.

- Teach bass and bass bar parts by rote and layer in with other two parts.

- Teach soprano xylophone part using body percussion with patschen with right hand moving over to outside of thigh when upper part moves to A and moving in to front of thigh on G. Transfer to instrument. (* patschen – rhythmically patting thighs)

- Teach glockenspiel part, which, requires students to divide notes up so all notes are played. Teach them how to play short glissandos up to the note (start a third below the note).

- Add a vocal that rhythmically matches the second part of the alto xylophone ostinato. Take care to prepare the part so students understand their notes are DIFFERENT than what was written for the instrument.

★ Discuss the importance of the instruments complementing the soloist, as the accompaniment could easily overpower the soloist. The class will notice this as they listen to the first presentation of the piece. They should discuss how to be sensitive to the soloists. At the same time the soloist needs to communicate how he or she wants the accompaniment to complement his or her improvisations. Present again and tape and review the work.

The Animals' Gifts

Track7

Kimberly McCord

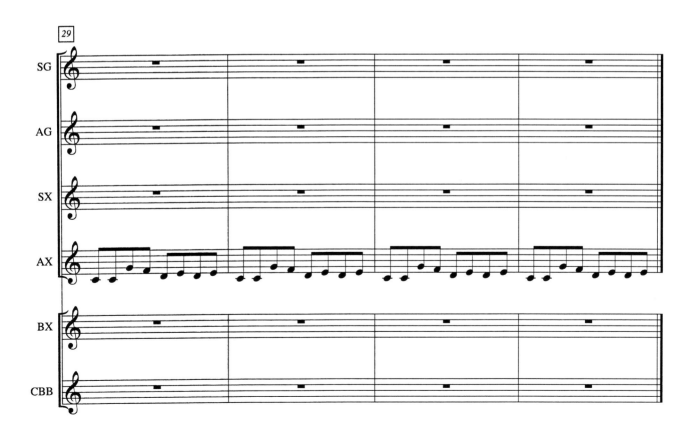

SCENE TWO

Zeus decides that there should be men on Earth (not women yet!). He calls Prometheus (in some versions it is Epimetheus that he calls; in others, it is both), and he orders him to go to Earth and create man. Prometheus completes the task, and asks Epimetheus to give man a gift. Epimetheus has no gifts left to give to man for protection. Prometheus decides that fire would be the best gift, but fire belongs to Zeus and is kept next to Zeus' throne. Zeus has made it very clear he will not share his fire. Epimetheus and Prometheus weigh the pros and cons of taking fire from Zeus. If they are caught, they could face severe punishment. If they do not give man fire, man might die. Epimetheus convinces Prometheus to take fire. He does and presents it to man.

DRAMA

+ Ask for two volunteers to improvise the first part of the scene when Zeus orders Prometheus to go to Earth and create man.

+ Elicit ideas from the class as to how Prometheus should create man. Does he create personalities (a shy one, a brave one, etc.), or types such as the hunter, the thinker, the musician, the builder, the healer, the artist, the teacher, etc.? Does he give each one a different look, height, etc.?

+ Select a group of six or more students to be "man," and have each of them sit in a special space as if they are a lump of clay. Prometheus will improvise dialogue as he brings man to life. Man (all students playing this role) will *slowly* come to life and explore the world they've never seen. Challenge the actors to use their five senses. What do they see, hear, feel, smell, taste (no cooked food!) in their new world? How many things can they do with their hands (clap, wave, etc.)? How many different ways can they move? Do they wobble at first? Skip? Jump? Allow time for them to act, and then instruct them to slowly sit in their space and rest.

+ Have Prometheus speak his thoughts about how he feels about his creation.

+ Ask for two volunteers to improvise the scene between Prometheus and Epimetheus as they try to figure out what gift to give man, since Epimetheus has none left. Discuss with the class why Prometheus decides on fire as the best gift for man. What is its usefulness to man? (warmth, light, to cleanse wounds, to cook, to make tools and inventions, to build homes and ships, to defend themselves, etc.) Challenge the students to convince and persuade as the two brothers debate about whether or not to take fire from Zeus, and who and how they should take it!

+ Elicit ideas from the class as to how Prometheus should take the fire. Does he ride in a chariot through the sky? Does he have someone else do it for him? Does he figure out a way for Zeus to be far away from his throne? Improvise their ideas.

+ Have another student role-play Prometheus, and a new group of six or more students role-play "man." Prometheus gives the fire to man, and delivers a speech to them about using the fire wisely, and the dangers of misuse. Instruct the students role-playing man to pantomime the uses of fire. Challenge them to use details and to really see each object. How do they make a fire to keep warm on a cold night? Do they gather wood first, etc.? How would they walk through unfamiliar territory using the fire as a torch to guide them, etc.?

- You can redo this scene with another group of students, and another Prometheus and Epimetheus with new ideas!

VOCAL Track 10

Since man has just been created and is speaking for the first time, it is a perfect opportunity to explore the sounds and rhythm involved in the jazzier side of vocal improvisation (scat).

- Review CD Tracks 4, 5, and 6 with your students.

- Lead the class in call and response for exercises 1 through 4 below, allowing students to echo the teacher's voice.

1. Practice common scat phrases and riffs:
- Bah-buh-doo-bop
- Beedle-ee-bop
- Sah-buh-dah-buh-dop
- Shay-bah-doo-bop
- Bah-doo-buh-dee

2. Now add "bah-doo-bah" between the phrases to connect them smoothly creating longer phrases and thoughts. Create original scat phrases with the class.

3. Speaking for the first time, the sounds can be more experimental and <u>vowel-centric</u> (**CD Track 10**).
- Ooo–ah
- Hey–ga
- Ooo–gah
- Gee–ah–kah
- Wah–dor–eh

4. Now, try combining the two different ways of scatting.
- Gee–ah–duh–bah
- Gee-dle–ee–gah
- Shoo–gah–bah
- Hey–goo–gah–dah
- Hee-dle –ooo–shah
- Wah–bah–dor–eh

Break up into small groups and encourage students to speak in scat and converse with one another. Give a speech using only scat. Recite a poem or familiar nursery rhyme in scat. Be expressive as you scat. Ask for soloists.

Refer to Vocal Warm-Ups: Combine the different sounds and create a chorus of scat.

SCENE THREE

Zeus discovers that someone dared to take his fire. He is furious. When he realizes it is Epimetheus and Prometheus, he sends for them. The two brothers try to reason with Zeus and make him understand that they took fire to help man. Zeus will not forgive them, and plans their punishment.

First he punishes Prometheus. He orders Hephaestus, the blacksmith - the artisan of the gods, to forge the heaviest of chains, and to chain Prometheus to a rock with a vulture guarding him. The vulture's job is to attack Prometheus' liver (which, because he is a Titan and immortal, miraculously grows back each time).

DRAMA

Ask for four students to role-play Zeus, Epimetheus, Prometheus, and Hephaestus. Have them:

+ Improvise the scene when Zeus discovers that someone has dared to steal fire from him. Challenge the student role-playing Zeus to capture the voice, body and movements of a powerful god who is so furious that his voice and actions are like thunder in the sky.

+ Improvise the scene when Epimetheus and Prometheus try to convince Zeus that they took fire to help man because he was weak and would die with no food, no light, no protection, etc. Prometheus might even try to convince Zeus that after all, it was Zeus who ordered man to be created, so didn't he want man to stay alive? Perhaps they challenge Zeus as to why he is reluctant to share his fire. Did he want man to be weak? To be no better than the animals? Was he afraid man would become powerful? *Zeus will not forgive them.*

+ Improvise the scene when Zeus orders Hephaestus to forge the chains.

+ Improvise in pantomime: Hephaestus forges the chains, chains Prometheus to a rock high above the Earth, and places a vulture nearby.

+ Pantomime Prometheus chained to the rock. (You can have a group of six or more students in special spaces play the role of Prometheus.) Instruct them to use their five senses and pantomime how they feel day after day, year after year, chained to the rock with a vulture attacking them daily. Have them feel the rough rock against their body; the wind in their face; the hot sun beating down on them; the rain on a cold stormy day. Have them look down at man on Earth using the fire wisely. Have them smell the food being cooked; taste the salt from the sea as the waves crash against the rocks; hear the waves beating against the rocks; man singing; etc.

+ Have another group of six or more students improvise the dialogue as Prometheus chained to the rock speaks his thoughts aloud. Was it worth it? Would man have been better off without fire? Was he being selfish? Why did Zeus tell him to create man and then not want to save man with fire? etc.

+ If you want to add a scene from another myth, you can improvise the scene years later when mighty Hercules arrives, destroys the vulture, and unchains Prometheus.

VOCAL AND INSTRUMENTAL

The vocal and instrumental activities provided here can be explored separately or easily combined to create an original musical composition with voice, body and hand drums.

+ The original composition can also serve as accompaniment for one of the suggested drama activities.

Vocal

+ Zeus is furious at Epimetheus and Prometheus for taking his fire. The students will need to make their voices sound furious.

+ What would make their voices sound furious? Refer to Vocal Warm-Ups for ideas. Low sound? High sound? Thunderous? Words? Body?

+ Refer to Vocal Warm-Ups: Combine the different sounds and create a chorus of fury.

Instrumental: Hand Drum Improvisation

+ Add hand drum improvisation to the scene to complement the drama and/or vocal.

+ Discuss with the students how and when to add hand drums to this scene.

+ Discuss with the students how the drums can combine with the vocals to create a furious musical composition.

+ Choose one of the suggested drama activities above and discuss how this composition can help dramatically.

Teaching Process

Model to students different ways to create sound on hand drums:

+ Playing 1/3 into the drum head area with two fingers

+ Playing with the flat part of the hand

+ Playing with one fingertip

+ Knocking on the outside rim of the drum

+ Taking the palm of the hand and rubbing in a circular motion across the drum head

+ Using a feather to play the drum

+ Dropping small beads on the drum head

+ Lightly pushing into the corner of the drum head after playing the drum to create a pitch that goes higher

+ Find other gentle ways to play hand drums

WHAT DOES FURY SOUND LIKE?

Action the sound is linked to	Sounds Used	Does the music complement the action? How?

- When animals are angry, what do they sound like?
- When the weather turns "angry" what does it sound like?

SCENE FOUR

Epimetheus receives his punishment. First, Zeus banishes Epimetheus from Mount Olympus, and sends him to live on Earth among men. Epimetheus tries to change Zeus' mind, but to no avail. Zeus orders Hephaestus to create a woman. Some stories say she was created out of clay; others out of fire; and others out of the opposites in the world. When she is completed, Zeus calls her Pandora, gift of all gifts. He gathers all the gods and goddesses, and instructs them to present Pandora with gifts before he brings her to life and gives her curiosity.

DRAMA

+ Have two students improvise the first part of the scene when Zeus banishes Epimetheus to Earth. Have Epimetheus try one last time to convince Zeus to let him remain on Mount Olympus, but to no avail.

+ Elicit ideas from the class as to how Pandora should be created, and improvise that scene.

+ Assign, or have each student select (or the classroom teacher can do this in preparation for this scene) a Greek god or goddess. Have each student gather information about the god or goddess, and decide what gift would be appropriate for that god or goddess to give to Pandora. For example, Athena, the goddess of wisdom, might give her wisdom; Poseidon, the god of the sea, might give her the ability to navigate the seas; Ares, the god of war, might give her the skills of a warrior; etc. They can also invent gods and goddesses such as Stone Hand, the god of sculpture who gives the gift of creativity, or the goddess of improvisation, who gives the ability to think quickly, etc.

+ Once the students have decided on a gift, act out the scene in the following way: 1) Zeus gathers the gods and goddesses, and asks them to give Pandora a gift before he brings her to life; 2) Each one arrives, tells Pandora who he/she is, and presents the gift however they decide.

+ They can speak, dance, sing, or use instruments as they present their gifts. They can deliver improvised speeches on how to use the gift, etc.

+ Challenge them to speak and move as their character. For example, how does the god of war move and speak? The goddess of grace and charm?

+ Improvise the end of the scene. Zeus brings Pandora to life (whoever plays Zeus can decide *how* he brings her to life, and improvise the dialogue as he gives her curiosity). Pandora comes to life and explores the world as a curious person.

VOCAL (Track 9)

- Familiarize the students with "Gifts from Gods and Goddesses" (**CD Track 9**).

- Explain to the students that there is music to be learned that will accompany their improvisations. Vocal improvisations will happen during the piece.

- Instruct the students to explore what gifts might be given: water, wind, music, etc.

- How would they make their voices sound like these gifts? High voice? Low voice? Loud? Soft? A whisper? Percussive? A combination? A pattern? (Refer to vocal Warm-Up section for ideas.)

- Teach the students the song. Follow the written teaching instructions and add the vocal improvisations at the correct time.

★ **Note:** You may have the students sing "Gifts from Gods and Goddesses" or use the accompanying CD, letting the students improvise with the recorded music.

SCENE FIVE

Zeus continues to execute his plan for Epimetheus' punishment. He calls Hermes, the messenger of the gods, and tells him to deliver Pandora, along with a box that he tells Hermes to give to Epimetheus, who is now living on Earth. Hermes is also to warn Pandora and Epimetheus **never to open the box or evil things will happen.** Every day Pandora becomes more and more curious about what is in the box. Epimetheus is convinced that the remainder of his punishment is in that box, because so far life on Earth is satisfactory. It is peaceful and good. Everyone is happy and healthy. He does not want to open the box.

DRAMA

- Ask for volunteers to improvise the beginning of the scene (Hermes, Zeus, Pandora, and Epimetheus, who is on Earth). Have the student who is playing Epimetheus decide what he is doing when Pandora is delivered, and how he reacts to his new present (Pandora) and the box.

- After Hermes leaves with his warning (the class can create haunting echoes of his warning), have students take turns as Pandora and Epimetheus, and convince each other to open or not to open the box. Challenge each pair to try different approaches as they persuade each other.

★ This sequence of persuading should be different than the Warm-Up, since they now know the context for the box.

Pandora's Box Scene 5
Gifts from Gods and Goddesses

Louise Rogers

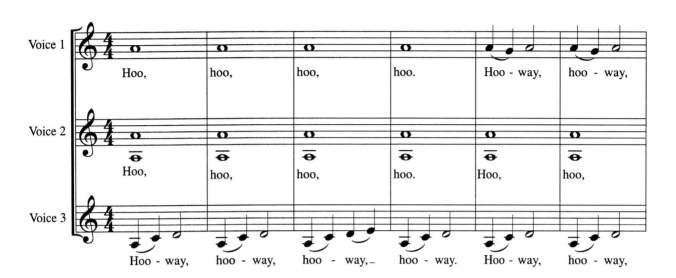

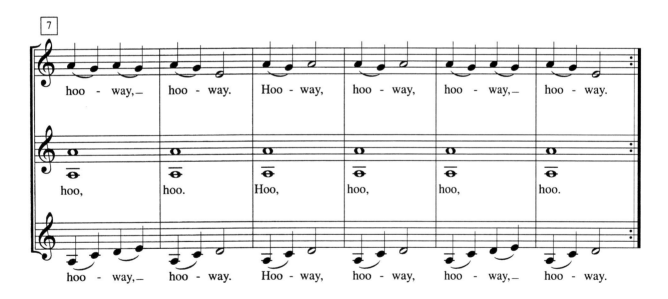

Teaching Process:
1. Teach Voice 3 first.
2. Add Voice 2, splitting the students in octaves in whichever range is most comfortable.
3. Add Voice 1.
4. Selected students improvise vocally over the choral section representing each gift.
   Singing continues until all of the gifts are given.
5. Improvise on pitched percussion or Orff setup in a minor pentatonic.

INSTRUMENTAL (Track 10)

Teaching Process - Minor

- Model soprano metallophone part by using a visual of notation of the four phrases. Play part again asking students to listen for phrases that are the same, different and similar. (Phrases 1 and 3 are the same, phrases 2 and 4 are different). Teach each phrase and then add together to make the entire melody.

- Teach bass xylophone/contrabass bar part through speech by having students chant "Do not look inside it. Do not look inside it."

- Transfer speech to patschen, both hands together on front of thigh for repeated section on words "Do not look in" and then move right hand to outside of thigh for 3rd measure when the E moves to F. This will transfer to the bass xylophone part and aid the student to understand that the right hand moves up to F on the notes that are played on outside of thigh.

- Transfer students who are able to successfully play the changing pitches to bass xylophone. If boomwhackers are used you will need to use two students to play this part, one on D and E and another on D and F.

- Add contrabass bar/bass boomwhackers to the same rhythm once the bass xylophone part is confident.

- Teach alto metallophone part through claps by adding claps as the bass parts play. Ask students to identify what word the claps play on (look).

- Add vibraslap part on final note.

Pandora's Box: Minor

 Track 10

Warm-Up

Kimberly McCord

- Teach bass xylophone/boomwhacker part through speech "Why not look inside it? Why not look inside it?"

- Transfer speech to patschen, both hands together on front of thigh for repeated section on words "Why not look in" and then move right hand to outside of thigh for 4th measure when the E moves to the F. This will transfer to the bass xylophone part and aid the student to understand that the right hand moves up to F♯ on the notes that are played on outside of thigh.

- Transfer students who are able to successfully play the changing pitches to bass xylophone. If boomwhackers are used you will need to use two students to play this part, one on D and E and another on D and F♯.

- Add contrabass bar/bass boomwhackers to the same rhythm once the bass xylophone part is confident.

- Prepare alto metallophone, soprano metallophone and glockenspiel parts by teaching three levels of body percussion occurring at the same time as the bass parts play. Alto is patschen, soprano is clap and glockenspiel is snap. Have students perform all levels of body percussion with bass part.

- Teach alto metallophone part through patschen as the bass parts play. Use front of thigh for first "why" and side of thigh for second "why" so students will see that the right hand moves up on second "why" which is similar to how bass parts were taught. Ask students to identify what word the pats came in on ("why").

- Transfer to instrument and layer in with bass parts.

- Teach soprano metallophone part using similar method as in previous parts.

- Transfer to instruments and layer with other parts.

- Glockenspiels play octave D's on snap part, transfer to instruments and layer with other parts.

- Add triangle and chime tree parts on the word "it."

Pandora's Box: Major
Warm-Up

Track 11

Arranged by
Kimberly McCord

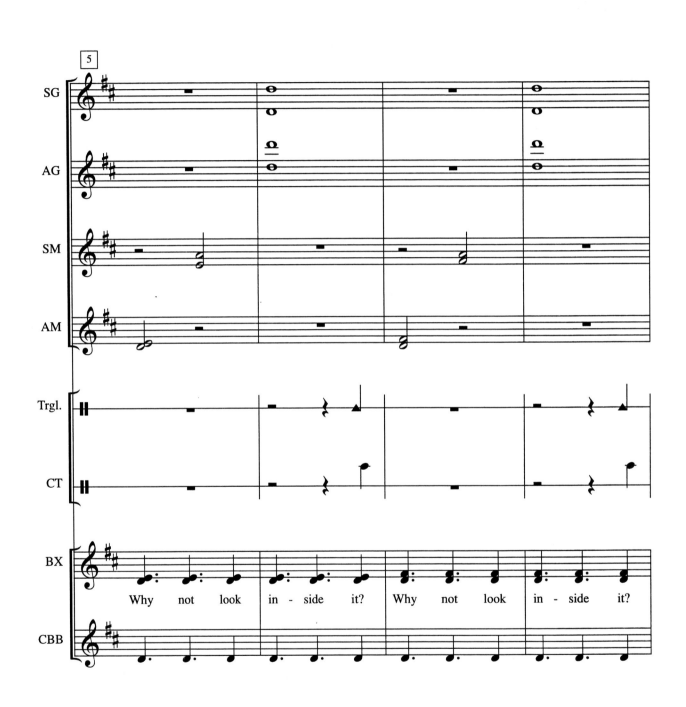

Why not look in - side it? Why not look in - side it?

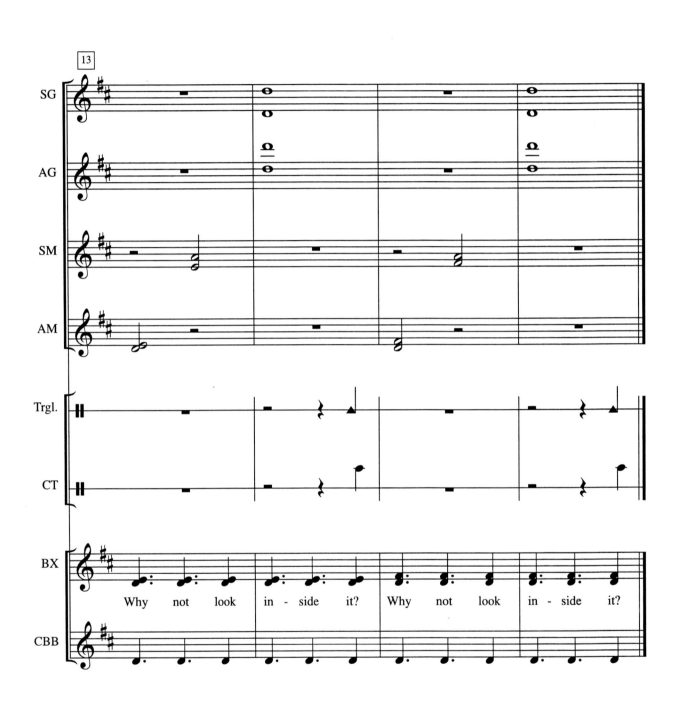

Does major mean hopeful and minor mean fear? Not all cultures hear major and minor tonalities the same. Be open to students deciding what mood they think major and minor represent. There isn't a right answer for this but the student decides what is the right answer. Encourage students to be creative and think like composers/improvisers as they decide how to make the music best represent what they hear in their heads.

SCENE SIX

One day Pandora is alone with the box. She promised Epimetheus that she would not open the box, yet Zeus gave her curiosity. Finally when her curiosity gets the best of her, she opens the box and all the evils (pain, disease, greed, gossip, violence, jealousy, lies, war, pollution, revenge, corruption, etc.) that are now in the world escape from the box. Pandora is terrified. She tries to get them back into the box, but it is too late.

DRAMA

Have the class generate a list of evils, including evil qualities in people, and then have each student or groups of students decide which evil they would like to represent. Also, select one student to role-play Pandora.

- Begin the scene with Pandora left alone with the box and her thoughts. Have the students in the class be her conscience and speak to her. Ask them to think about what they could say or do to stop someone from doing something that is dangerous or wrong. After each student has spoken as a conscience, have half the class tempt her with "Open it," and the other half, "Do not open it." Have them speak all at the same time, getting louder and louder until you signal them to fade into a whisper as they await Pandora's decision. Does she open it slowly? Peek first? Do the evils whisper, "Let us out," while she makes her decision?

- Have each student find a special space. When Pandora opens the box, each student, one at a time (or group of students if there are more than one portraying the same evil) comes out of the imaginary box and: 1) *freezes* like a statue of that evil; 2) slowly comes to life, makes the sounds of that evil; 3) state what evil he/she is; and 4) describes what he/she is going to cause to happen as it escapes into the world. *They can speak, sing or dance this*!

Note: Challenge them to use their faces, voices and bodies to really become the evil they are portraying. Long scarves or large pieces of fabric work well here.

- At some point during the escape of the evils, Epimetheus returns. Have a student improvise his reaction. Does he try to get some of the evils back into the box? Is he scratched, stung, hurt, etc? Does he scold Pandora?

- After all the evils escape, focus on a scene between Pandora and Epimetheus. How do they feel? Improvise the dialogue.

VOCAL  Track 12

"Pandora's Box Is Opened"

- Explain to the students that there is music to be taught and sung that will accompany their improvisations.

- Familiarize students with "Pandora's Box Is Opened" (**CD Track 12**).

- Instruct the students to use their voices to be the ills of the world: pain, disease, greed, gossip, violence, jealousy, lies, war, pollution, etc.

- Encourage students to utilize all of the sounds they have explored: high voice, low voice, high and low mixed, loud, soft, angry, furious, percussive, or any combination.

- Teach the students the song. Follow the written instructions to the music and add the vocal improvisations at the correct time.

Pandora's Box Is Opened

Louise Rogers

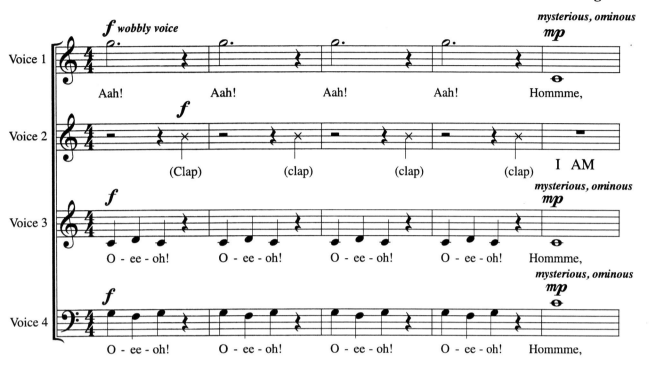

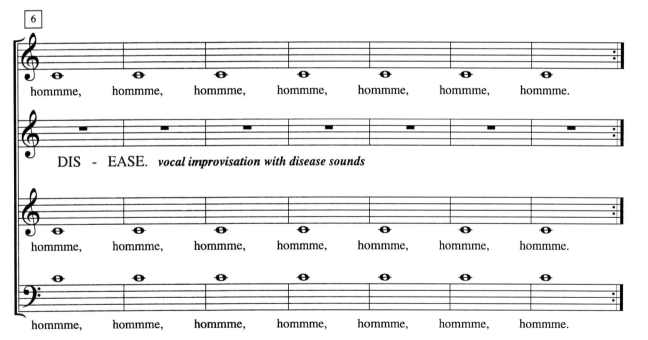

Notes

The box is opened and all of the ills of the world are released. The ills of the world should be decided upon before starting the piece. The ills of the world are represented by vocal or body percussion sounds.

Teaching Process

1. Teach Voice 3 first.
2. Add Voice 4.
3. Add Voice 1.
4. Add Voice 2. Clap occurs when other parts rest. Layer in improvised evil sounds

Note: You may have the students sing "Pandora's Box Is Opened" or use the accompanying CD, letting the students improvise with the recorded music.

Activity Extension: Students may also write lyrics. Their classroom teacher can work on original poems and they can set the lyrics to the accompanying music and sing or read these as they come out of the box. If sung, accompanying music can easily accommodate short phrases and longer poems.

If the class is working with the accompanying CD, they will need to be sure that their poem or phrase fits in the allotted time of eight measures.

FINAL SCENE

Pandora and Epimetheus are hurt. They've been stung, scratched, etc. Just when they think there is no hope, they hear a very soothing, gentle voice begging to be let out of the box. At first they are hesitant, but whatever is in the box convinces them that it is not like the evils that escaped. They decide to release the last thing in the box. Carefully, they open the box, and out comes Hope, who explains to them that although there will always be evil in the world, there will also always be hope.

DRAMA

+ Have all the students *freeze* in special spaces as the evils they represent, so that an atmosphere of doom and evil permeates the room. Ask for a volunteer (or more) to be the voice in the box begging to be let out.

+ Have two volunteers role-play Epimetheus and Pandora, and discuss whether or not to let this last creature out of the box. The class can chant, "Keep the box closed" or "Open it and see what's in there."

+ Discuss with the class what it means to be hopeful, and have a student improvise the dialogue as Hope comes out of the box.

+ Ask the class how they would like to end the story. Does Hope move in and around the evils? Does she take Pandora and Epimetheus by the hand and leave? etc.

INSTRUMENTAL/VOCAL   🎵 Track 13

+ Familiarize the students with "Hope" (**CD Track 13**).

+ Explain to the students that there is music to be learned that will accompany their improvisations. Vocal and instrumental improvisations will happen during the piece.

+ Encourage students to find beauty in their voices and in the instruments. What is a beautiful sound? An angel? A bird? The ocean? A light rain? The wind? A combination of sounds? Create a list of beautiful sounds.

+ How would they make their voices sound beautiful? High voice? Low voice? Loud? Soft? A whisper? Percussive? A combination? A pattern? (Refer to vocal Warm-Ups section for ideas.)

- Choose instruments to make beautiful sounds.

- Teach the students the song. Follow the written teaching instructions to the music and add the vocal improvisations at the correct time.

- You may have the students sing "Hope" or use the accompanying CD letting the students improvise with the recorded music.

Teaching Process:

- Teach voice part 3.

- Teach voice part 2.

- Teach voice part 1.

- Dynamics are the focus of this piece. Sing "Hope" using the dynamics indicated on the music.

- How do the dynamics help to demonstrate the mood of hope? If the music had improvisation in it do you think it would strengthen or weaken the sound of hope?

- Add vocal or instrumental improvisations to the beginning and/or the end of the piece.

Optional Orff Parts:

- Teach contrabass bars part first.

- Bass Metallophone, Alto Metallophone and Soprano Metallophone parts are all with voice parts.

- Glock parts should be added last.

- Layer each part in with entire ensemble one part at a time.

- If you do not have metallophones, xylophones can be substituted if students can play soft rolls to sustain the notes.

- If you do not have contrabass bars, do not substitute another instrument.

- Experiment with different arrangements of the piece. Perhaps begin with only voices, then repeat with only instruments, and finally finish with both instruments and voices. Students can decide on the arrangement.

Pandora's Box
Hope

Music by: Louise Rogers
Arranged by: Louise Rogers
Orff arrangment: Kimberly McCord

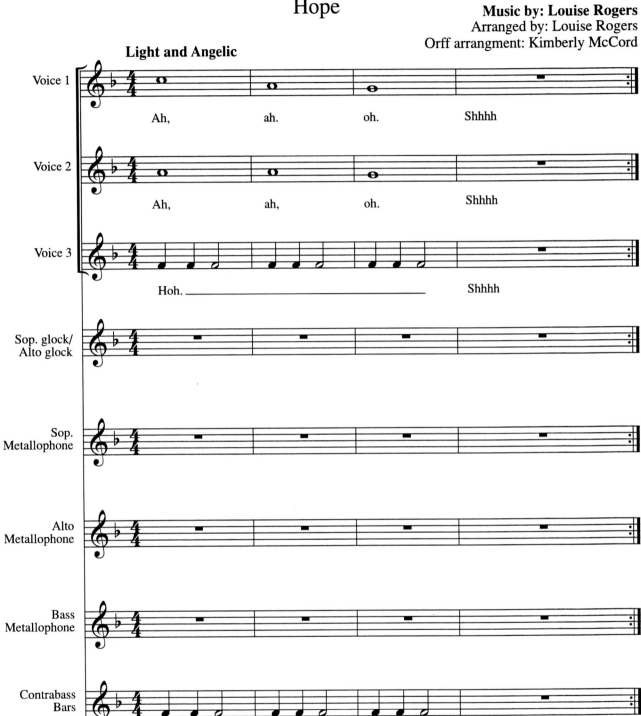

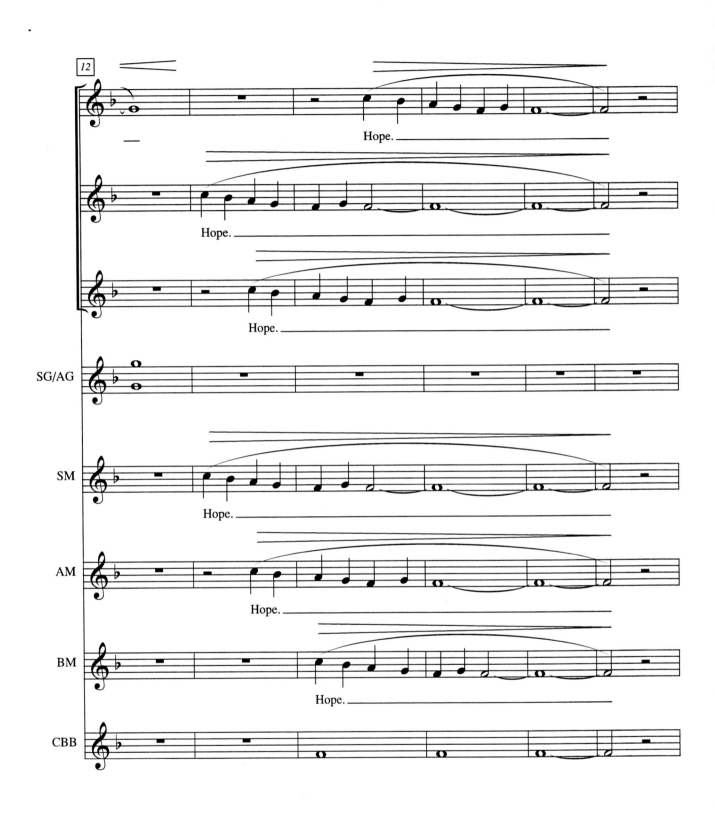

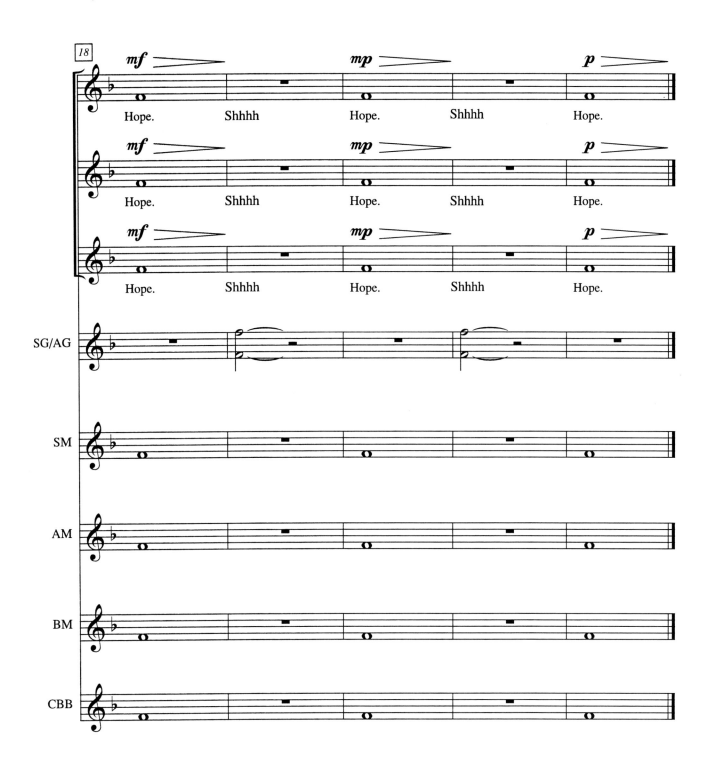

CREATIVE EXTENSIONS

DRAMA

+ At the end of the story, Pandora can deliver an improvised speech of apology.

+ Ask students what gift they would have given to man. Why? They can write/improvise that story.

+ Students can imagine they are reporters and interview characters in the story, or report on each of the major news stories in the myth.

+ Ask students what else could have been in the box. How would that have changed the story and the world? The class can create an original myth about how evil came into the world. You can do this as a circle story (one person starts the story, and then the next one adds to the story) or in groups.

+ The class can have a trial to determine if it is anyone's fault. Is it Pandora for opening the box? Zeus for giving Pandora curiosity or for not wanting to share his fire with man? Prometheus for disobeying Zeus and stealing the fire? Epimetheus for not stopping Pandora? Anyone else?

+ Read and improvise other cultures' myths about how evil came into the world.

+ Ask students what they would like to see come out of a box *now* that would change the world. They can write or improvise that story.

MUSIC

+ If this were a myth from another culture, what might the music sound like? What type of animals would be included, etc.? Would the evils be different or are they universal?

IT COULD ALWAYS BE WORSE

Objectives

- Students will recognize and understand the four basic elements of a story: character, plot, setting, theme

- Students will develop original stories alone and in groups

- Students will express story themes and characterization through improvisation in music and drama

- Students will know the structure and elements of a folktale

- Students will create tableaux that capture the theme of a scene

- Students will add scenes and characters to the original story in order to bring to life a village long ago and far away

- Students will develop an appreciation and understanding of how a folktale reflects a culture

- Students will collaborate and select characters, settings, and best ways to dramatize a scene

- Students will hone their pantomime skills, and express themselves non-verbally

- Students will develop improvisations into scenes for shared performances

- Students will demonstrate an understanding of the characters they portray by creating appropriate dialogue and using appropriate voices, body movement and gestures

- Students will collaborate to establish playing spaces for their dramatizations, select props, and utilize the space for staging

- Students will work to express the themes, plot, characters and settings through music (instrumental and vocal) and drama, and understand how each art form enhances a scene

- Student will evaluate their improvisations and try alternate ways to develop each scene and solve each conflict

- Students will perform expressively on instruments

- Students will sing expressively

- Students will improvise and perform alone and in groups

- Students will develop arrangements of pieces they learn to play or sing

- Students will learn Klezmer music and songs that reflect the culture of the folktale

National Standards for Theatre: Standard #1, 2, 3, 4, 6, 7

National Standards for Music: #1, 2, 3, 4, 6, 7, 8, 9

Materials

- Versions of the folktale
- Boomwhackers, hand drums, recorders, soprano, alto, bass metallophones, soprano, alto, bass xylophones, contra bass bars, soprano and alto glockenspiels, triangle, chime tree. Some of these instruments can be substituted with boomwhackers or pieces can be performed without Orff instruments (see specific pieces for ideas).

Prior Knowledge

- Students are familiar with the definition of *improvisation* in music and drama

- Students are familiar with the definition of a folktale

- Students are familiar with the definition of *pantomime* and *role-playing*

- Students know how to play various unpitched percussion instruments

- Students know how to play Orff instruments

INTRODUCTION TO THE UNIT

Explain to the class that in this unit they will explore a Russian/Yiddish (Jewish) folktale, *It Could Always Be Worse*. The tale takes place in a town in Eastern Europe in the late 19th century.

Discuss the elements of a folktale and oral tradition, or work collaboratively with the classroom teacher and librarian to introduce or review the elements of a folktale. We suggest working on this unit when the classroom teacher and/or librarian are reading and studying folktales.

There are two basic elements of a folktale that are important for them to know prior to beginning the activities:

- A folktale reflects a country and culture. The dwellings, animals, chores, food, customs, holidays, characters, wise person, etc. are different, depending on the origin of the story. In this story, for example, the wise person is a Rebbe (Rabbi).

- A folktale does not have a specific author. It is handed down through the years, many times in the oral tradition, and retold differently by different people. There are many versions of the story we're exploring.

★ We recommend Margot Zemach's version of the folktale "It Could Always Be Worse." Other versions are listed at the end of the unit.

IMPROVISATIONAL WARM—UPS

TO PREPARE FOR THE STORY AND GENERATE AN INTEREST IN THE STORY

Review *audience rule, freeze and focus, improvisation, pantomime, role-playing,* and *special space.*

WARM-UP #1

DRAMA

Storytelling

Warm-Up for the story with creative storytelling related to the theme, "It Could Always Be Worse."

Have the class sit in a circle. One student will improvise the beginning of a story with the line, "You'll never believe what happened to me!" At some point, stop the storyteller by saying, *It could be worse.* The next person will continue to improvise the story and *make it worse.* Each time you say, *It could be worse,* the next person adds to the story and makes it worse. The last person in the circle will conclude the story. The story can be real or fantasy.

Note: Challenge the students to end their stories creatively, rather than having someone die.

For example:

Real:

"You'll never believe what happened to me today! I overslept, but when I jumped out of bed to get ready, I tripped over books on the floor, and twisted my wrist. I turned on the water to wash my face, and it was ice cold. I opened a package of cereal, and it spilled. I rushed to clean it up, and spilled the milk (*It could be worse!*). I got to my car and my car wouldn't start, so I was late for school (*It could be worse!*). I rushed to find my class, and discovered it was picture day. As I smiled for the camera, I realized I was wearing two different color socks, and I had a hole in my sweater, and (*It could be worse!*), etc."

or

Fantasy:

"You'll never believe what happened to me today! I auditioned for the lead role in the school musical play. I started to sing, but no sound came out of my mouth (or only gibberish sounds escaped, or multi-colored bubbles, etc.). So, I decided to audition for the dance team, but I tripped on my shoelace and landed in the orchestra pit (*It could be worse!*). So, I decided to be in the orchestra, but as I blew on my trombone, rainbows (or animal sounds or bubbles) came out (*It could be worse!*), etc."

Complete several circle stories with a different student starting each story.

Once students are comfortable improvising stories as a group, ask for volunteers who would like to improvise an entire story by him/herself. Students can make up their own story starter, or you can compile cards with a suggestion on each card. A student selects a card, reads the situation, and improvises the story.

Some suggested story starters:

You'll never believe what happened to me today!
+ I spilled glue on the collage I spent two weeks creating.
+ Today I missed the school bus, so I had to walk to school. It started to snow (*real*), or there was this tiny alien creature zipping up and down the sidewalk (*fantasy*).
+ I woke up this morning and all I could do was sing.
+ My saxophone only played flute music.
+ My drumsticks started to dance across my drum.
+ My music teacher turned into me, and I turned into my music teacher.
+ There was a family of mice in the piano, and every time I played, only squeaks came out.
+ A UFO landed in my back yard.
+ I was glued to a chair.
+ I tried to walk on the ceiling.
+ I traveled to the moon.
+ I had breakfast with the President of the United States.
+ I walked in my sleep, and ate all the candy at the candy store.
+ My computer (or video game) came to life.
+ I was sucked into my computer (or video game).

- I became a dinosaur.
- I was the lawyer for the giant in "Jack and the Beanstalk."
- A giant asked me to let him live in my backyard.
- A humongous turtle was swimming in my bathtub.
- I woke up and all I could do is.....
- I kissed my favorite movie or rock star.
- I woke up and discovered I was invisible.
- I made friends with an elephant.
- I was attacked by a cactus plant.
- I flew off my roof and landed across the United States (or in a jungle, or any other place).
- I turned into the instrument I was playing (or the pet I was feeding, or the character in the book I was reading, etc.).
- I was hugged by a giant octopus.
- It was raining M&M candies.
- Etc.

★ You may need to side coach in order to keep each story moving towards a conclusion. You can interject *"It can always be worse!"* to motivate a student to move to the next part of the improvised story. Set a timer, or signal each student when it is time to conclude. Have fun creating your own story starters, and elicit ideas from students.

Refer to page 286 in Milton Polsky's book, *Let's Improvise*, and the TMATTY's in Maria C. Novelly's book, *Theatre Games for Young Performers* for additional story starters.

★ You can do the above activity with a competitive edge. The class votes on which story was the worse-case scenario.

VOCAL  Track 14

"Things Could Be Worse Blues"

This vocal Warm-Up relates to the previous drama Warm-Up. It makes sense to sing the blues after the class has been introduced to the concepts explored in the drama Warm-Up. This is the perfect opportunity to introduce the blues to the class.

Before class, refer to the "Story Starters" that the class created in Drama Warm-Up #1. Explain to the class that they will write a blues song with some of the ideas that they have created. They can create the blues as a story from beginning to end, or write several separate verses.

Creating the verse with the rhyming scheme:

Tell the class to start with the phrase, "I woke up this morning."

Ask them to finish the sentence. What happened next? Remind them that it has to be bad, and it will only get worse!

Sample:

I woke up this mornin' —and I was glued to my bed.

(this verse always repeats)

I woke up this morning—and I was glued to my bed.

(Now, the last word of the next phrase must rhyme with last word of the phrase before which was "bed." Ask the class to finish the thought)

I was glued to my bed—couldn't even move my head!

First let's learn the melody. See written music and sample verse to help get the class started.

A blues accompaniment has been provided on the enclosed CD. After the class has created their verses and learned the melody, have them sing along with the CD.

 Track 15

Things Could Be Worse Blues

Louise Rogers

Change the rhythm when needed to accommodate original lyrics.

Sample verse
I woke up this mornin'
And I was glued to the bed
I woke up this mornin'
And I was glued to the bed
I was glued to the bed
Couldn't even move my head!

Then along came my cat
And he tickled my toes
Then along came my cat
And he tickled my toes
He tickled my toes
Then he licked my nose!

Verses can be separate entities **or be** a story from beginning to end.

INSTRUMENTAL ⊙ Track 16

"Surprise Me!"

What could be more surprising than waking up and finding out you were invisible or that a cactus plant was attacking you?! Surprise is an important element of improvisation. Improvisation should be like playing, full of delight and surprise.

Improvising is like playing with some of the best toys you can imagine. The problem with toys is after a while they get boring, break, or you outgrow them. Improvising never gets boring, because it is always new and different, and best of all you use your imagination! Improvising is especially fun when you get to improvise with someone who has a good imagination. You never know what they will play or sing, and what they do can inspire you to go in a musical direction you never would have imagined.

Sometimes musicians like to musically play with sound toys and see what ideas emerge from the fun. You're going to create sound toys and try to surprise your improvising partner.

Teaching Process

+ Students will improvise short phrases of 4 or 8 measures using an adapted Klezmer mode (C, D, F♯, G, A, B♭, C), see p.57. At the end of each improvised phrase the soloist will insert a musical surprise. The soloist that follows will end their phrase with something that uses an element of the idea the previous soloist used for a surprise. For example, the first soloist may decide to end their phrase with a loud, high note. The second soloist may decide to end with a loud, low note or a soft, high note. The third soloist starts the game over.

+ First, teach all students the notes on recorder for the adapted Klezmer mode (see written out mode in the recorder part for "Surprise Me!"). Play short patterns that students echo back to you (see "Surprise Me!" phrases). Ask what note is left out (E).

+ Next, play call and response patterns. One person plays a short phrase and another plays an answer using only notes from the Klezmer mode.

+ Finally, have students play patterns again, but this time ending their phrase with a surprise. Ask how they can create a musical surprise. Some possible ideas are using high and low pitches, dynamics, changing timbre by half-holing a note (partially covering a note but not completely), putting in a rest, playing fast or slow, or doing something totally unexpected like singing or stomping a foot.

+ Teach the bass and alto xylophone parts first using the chant "Sur-prise me!" then transferring the chant to leg pats. Perform two patterns by patting on outside of left thigh and inside of right thigh and two patterns of center left thigh and center right thigh. This will help students to transfer to changing notes on the instruments. When the syncopated rhythm is solid, transfer a few students to bass and alto xylophones. Students will play long F♯ and A two patterns and then move to long G and B♭ for two patterns then back to F♯ and A. Avoid using metallophones because the sound will become too sustained.

- Teach tambourine part first by clapping on counts two and four with the bass and alto part playing at the same time. This is a challenging part because the player will need to be independent of the syncopated accompaniment in the xylophones.

- Perform "Surprise Me!" with improvised recorder and soprano xylophone parts. Students can decide if they want to have partners play the same instrument or different instruments.

Adapted Klezmer Mode

Surprise Me!

Kimberly McCord

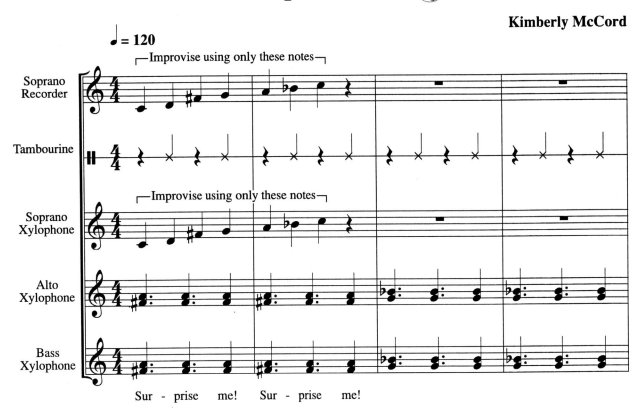

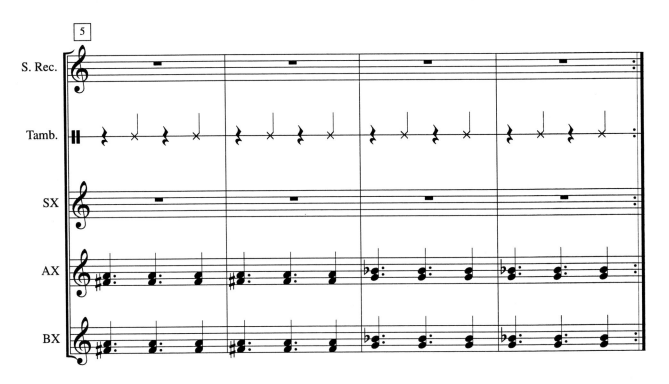

WARM-UP #2

Summarize the plot of *It Could Always Be Worse*, but do not give away the ending, which contains the solution to the problem. Explain that in this folktale there is a family who lives in an overcrowded hut with limited space. Everyone fights and complains. Grandma snores, animals are underfoot, someone is always hogging blankets, etc. One day when the wife can no longer tolerate the chaos, she pleads with her husband to seek advice from the wise person, who in this village is the Rebbe.

Show the class an illustration from Margot Zemach's version of the story, so they have a sense of the hut, characters, and the crowded situation.

DRAMA

Tableau

Divide the class into groups of 4-8 students. Instruct each group to collaborate and compose a tableau (or whatever you prefer to call it....a still life, painting, photo) of the family in the crowded house. Allow time for each group to decide on a specific title.

Some suggestions: *Too Noisy. No Room to Study or Sing. Where's the Cat? Whose Turn to Change the Baby's Diaper? Bedtime With No Blankets. Dinner Time Chaos. Too Many Chores. Trapped. Who Sleeps With Grandma? Stop Snoring! I Will Not Share My Cookie. Tired Mother*, etc.

+ Once they decide on a specific title, each student decides on a specific character (human or animal, age and personality). The group then decides how they want to arrange themselves as a photo to convey the title.

+ After each tableau is presented, ask the class to guess what the title is, based on the arrangement of the characters, and their expressions, gestures, and dialogue.

VOCAL Track 17

Explain to the class that they will create their own crowded house scenario.

+ "Debka Hora" is a rhythmic Israeli dance and round. It is sung on "lah" as people dance and clap. Learn the song. Add clapping and foot tapping on beats 1 and 2. Once the class is comfortable with the song, introduce the concept of the round. Explain to the class that they will divide into groups and start singing the song at different times. Remind them to concentrate on their part and don't let the other singers confuse them! Singers can enter every four measures, or you can break it up into two sections: the first four measures and the second four measures (keeping the repeats).

+ Our crowded house is filled with singers and dancers. Unfortunately, the mother is trying to read while the kids practice their song. Ask for a small group of volunteers—about eight is a good number. If they want to work in pairs, then you will need a larger group of volunteers. Assign each volunteer (or group) a character. For example, the mother (who is quiet for the entire scene), the father, all of the brothers and sisters, and perhaps even the family cat or dog.

- Set the scene of your crowded house by placing the characters in designated spaces. Start your crowded house with the mother sitting quietly reading her book and drinking her tea. As you point to the characters, they will begin to sing, and as each character starts to sing, the house becomes more chaotic and noisy, making it impossible for the mother to read! The singers get more excited and each group begins clapping and foot tapping. Even the dog and cat "woof" and "meow" in song. Encourage the class to add movement by turning in circles, clapping their partners hands, holding hands with their partner and turning in a circle. However, remind them to stay within their designated spaces and be mindful of the round. As the teacher, if you time the entrances correctly, you will create a very musically chaotic, crowded house! To end this chaos, one by one, point to each group or person to indicate *stop*. "Ahh," the mother sighs, takes a sip of her tea and can finally read again .... until the next group of volunteers!

Debka Hora   Track 17

INSTRUMENTAL

We will be exploring the use of call and response and creating tension in improvised solos in this unit.

- Download or find a copy of the piece, "Klezmer" by Steve Hudson's Outer Bridge Ensemble (available on iTunes). This recording is rather long, 6 minutes and 20 seconds. It might work best to listen through the violin solo and pause the music at the saxophone solo. Have students write answers on the worksheet that is provided. After answers have been recorded, discuss with the class what they wrote and then finish listening to the saxophone solo and the end of the piece. Allow students to record their answers and discuss what they wrote. Both solos and accompaniment are very different and should provide good contrast and opportunities to compare and think about how two different instruments and soloists approach the same music.

- This music is not traditional Klezmer music but is more jazz-based. Traditional Klezmer music will be included later in this unit but this music is more closely related to the call and response music we will develop.

- Extension: Ask students to figure out the melody part of "Klezmer" on their recorders.

Listening to "Klezmer"

First improvised solo - violin
How does the violin create interest in the solo? Is there tension in the solo? What does the soloist do to create tension?

How does the group accompany the soloist? What do they do to support the soloist?

Second improvised solo - alto saxophone
How does the violin create interest in the solo? Is there tension in the solo? What does the soloist do to create tension?

How does the group accompany the soloist? What do they do to support the soloist?

Have you heard music like this before?

WARM-UP #3

Explain that in this folktale, the family constantly argues. There are conflicts between parents, parents and grandparents, parents and children, siblings, and maybe even the animals! Discuss whether the types of arguments and conflicts are different long ago and far away than they are now, or if there are conflicts that transcend time and place (i.e., a child wants to go somewhere but a parent says no; someone wants to avoid a chore; one sister wants to borrow an article of clothing from another, etc.). Point out that what might differ is the *type* of clothing one wants to borrow, or the *type* of chore, or *where* the teen might want to go.

DRAMA

Conflict Improvisations

- Begin with a focus on *present day* conflicts. Have each student select a partner and decide on something they would argue about in their home (who walks the dog; who baby-sits; a curfew time; child wants to go somewhere and parent says no; etc.). Explain that they are NOT to argue yet. They are only to decide on the idea for the conflict.

- Have each pair find a special space, and at a signal from you, everyone will argue simultaneously *without words*. Challenge them to use only facial expressions and gestures. Remind them to listen for the *freeze* signal. Signal to begin, allow time for the arguments, and then call *freeze*.

- Focus now on one pair at a time, but explain that this time when you point to each pair, they will speak, but they must *persuade* and *convince* each other. They can't yell or argue. They must give reasons and think of a variety of ways to solve the conflict. As you point to each pair (one pair at a time), they begin the improvisation.

★ You can let these Warm-Ups be brief, or you can re-do them and have students in each pair reverse roles.

VOCAL  Track 18

"Debka Hora: Moods"

Living in a crowded house can certainly put even the most cheerful person in a bad mood at times! Remind the students of the conflicts discussed in Drama Warm-Up #3.

The characters in the crowded house use their voices to show emotion. Just by the sound of the voice, we know if a person is sad or happy, excited or bored, tired or energetic, wise or silly, sweet or mean, or angry or content. Sometimes the voice can even be persuasive.

This activity can be done with a partner or in two groups. Review (or learn) the song "Debka Hora." Ask for volunteers and explain that they will sing the song in a call and response style following the directions on the music. Decide on a conflict. Will they argue? Persuade? Perhaps one group is happy and the other group is sad. Is one child (group) making fun of another? How is the other responding? Is there a bully? Explore all of the different emotions that the voice has to offer, and sing "Debka Hora" in this voice. Encourage the singers to change the consonants and vowels to fit the emotion. For example, "heh," "weh," or "zee" instead of "lah."

Debka Hora: Moods

INSTRUMENTAL ⟨Track 16⟩

"Surprise Me!" with melody

+ Teach the melody on recorder and soprano xylophone for "Surprise Me!" Students should decide on an arrangement of "Surprise Me!" including how to start and end the piece; how many times to play the melody; which instruments play the melody; and how many call and response "Surprise Me!" solos to incorporate. After the solos, the melody should return.

+ Perform the piece with the solos.

+ Ask students to assess their performance including the effectiveness of their arrangement. Did the arrangement sound the way they thought it would? Is there anything they would do differently? Incorporate a few suggestions and try the piece again. Students might choose to change parts since the accompaniment parts do not get to solo or play the melody.

The melody is similar but not the same as "Klezmer" by Steve Hudson's Outer Bridge Ensemble.

WARM-UP #4

Remind the class that this folktale takes place on a farm long ago and far away in a country that no longer exists. Discuss the animals that are on a farm, and the chores this family completes inside and outside the house (scatter seeds, feed the chickens, milk the cow, carry pails of water, hang clothes to dry, peel onions, slice carrots, knead dough, scrub the floor, wash dishes, etc.).

DRAMA

Review or introduce *pantomime* (refer to the introduction to this book) and *special space.*

+ Have students find a special space, and have each student decide on an *inside* chore to pantomime. Challenge them to think of at least five details involved in performing that chore. For example, if they peel onions, do they wash and peel them first? What kind of utensil do they use? Do their eyes tear, etc.?

+ Allow time for them to pantomime, and then ask them to pantomime the same chore with an emotion. Are they happy? Ill? Angry with their sister because it was her turn? Disappointed because they wanted to go with a friend to town? Proud because Mom assigned them the hardest chore?

+ Allow time for them to pantomime, and then have them decide on an *outside* chore. Again, focus them on the details involved in performing that chore and how they feel. This time, have them also consider the weather. Is it cold, hot, rainy, sunny or stormy? Allow time to pantomime.

+ Have students decide on any chore (*inside* or *outside*) and then perform that chore with an obstacle. For example, how do you mop the floor if the cat keeps walking on it? How do you hang clothes to dry if the wind keeps blowing them off the line, and they land on the goat's horns? How do you pluck feathers off the chicken if you are allergic or have a cold and keep sneezing? How do you open a pickle jar if the cap is stuck? How do you slice carrots if you cut your finger? How do you change a baby's diaper if the baby is squirming? How do you fill a bucket with water if there's a small hole in the bucket? How do you hammer a crate if you can't find the right size nail? etc. **Note to teacher:** You can do this obstacle activity in three ways: 1) Have the entire class pantomime each of the above suggested actions simultaneously, first without the obstacle, and then with the obstacle. 2) Each student decides on a specific action and in a special space pantomimes that action and then adds the obstacle 3) Divide the class into groups of 2-4. Each pair or group decides on an action and an obstacle, and presents it to the class. The class guesses the action and the obstacle.

"Debra Hora: Obstacles"

Explain that the characters in the crowded house face obstacles while doing their chores, and now we're going to face some obstacles with singing!

♦ Review (or learn) "Debka Hora: Obstacles" (**CD Track 19**). See written music below. Some examples of vocal obstacles have been added. After the class has explored these obstacles, generate a list of other vocal obstacles and replace the written obstacles with the students' original ideas.

♦ After everyone has the hang of it, you can change the placement of the obstacles. For example, the class would sing the first two notes and then you announce, "Yawn!" The class then stops to yawn until you cue them back in. This adds the element of surprise and is a lot of fun!

♦ Remind the students that it takes a lot of concentration to get back on track after encountering an obstacle, and often requires some quick thinking.

 Track 19

Debka Hora: Obstacles

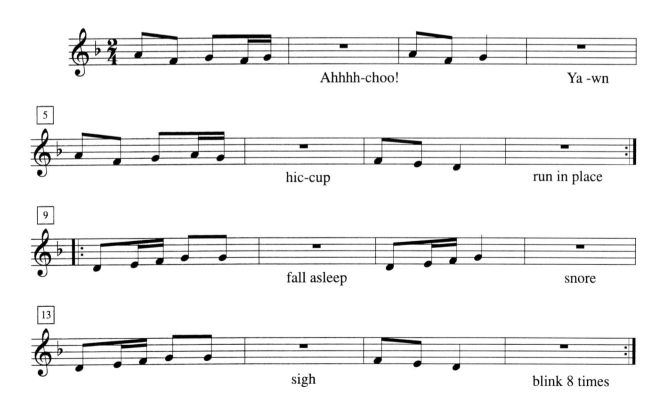

INSTRUMENTAL (Track 16)

"Surprise Me!" with solos expressing mood

In Drama Warm-Up #4, the pantomimes expressed mood. Sometimes the mood was anger, frustration, disappointment, or some other feeling as a result of the chore, weather or other circumstance. Moods can be expressed in solos too.

Teacher Directions

- Have students choose a mood to surprise the class with, and see if they can figure out how to show that through your solo.

- Have students perform two solos (a call and response) using "Surprise Me!" melody and accompaniment. Then stop the group and see if they can guess what the two moods were. Ask the students the following questions: "What in the music helped to convey the mood?" "How did the soloist create that mood on the instrument?" "What ideas do you have that you would have used to create that mood?"

- Select two students to go next that are going to play two NEW moods. See if students can identify the moods, and lead them through the above questions again.

- Continue with new partners.

CORE ACTIVITIES

★ Since this is a folktale, the characters have no specific names. Perhaps the classroom teacher and librarian could involve the class in a study of names that are indigenous to certain cultures. What would be an appropriate name for the father in this Russian/Jewish tale? (Mendel, Sol, Daniel, Rubin, Nathan, Tevye, Noah, etc.) The wife? (Sadie, Leah, Rivka, Bella, Golde, Hannah, Esther, Rachel, Sarah, Rebecca, etc.) You might want to establish names for the characters instead of referring to them as "the poor man," "his wife," "his children," etc. We have chosen Mendel and Sadie, but the class can decide on names.

SCENE ONE

Introduce the class to the beginning of the story: *A very poor family (a husband, his wife, his mother, and six children) live in an overcrowded, noisy, small hut in a small village. At any given time, there are cries, arguments, and complaints. Even the animals join the chorus of woeful sounds.*

DRAMA

+ Ask for 8-10 volunteers (when they finish, another group of 8-10 will improvise), and have each volunteer select a partner. Each pair is to decide who they are (animal, parent, aunt, uncle, sibling, cousin who stopped in for a visit, etc.); where they are (inside, outside, under the bed); and a conflict that would be appropriate for long ago, far away, and specific to this culture. Instruct them not to have the argument yet. As they plan, it is a good idea for you to check with each pair to make certain they can state their conflict, character, and where they are.

Some suggestions:
+ Who sleeps on the top bunk or with grandma who snores?
+ Who gets the pillow tonight?
+ Who peels the onions prior to going to school?
+ Who gets into the warm bath first?
+ You want to be a singer, but your father wants you to be a learned scholar.
+ Your brother, the scholar, is trying to study, but you want to practice your singing part for the play at the synagogue (or practice blowing the shofar, or playing the fiddle).
+ In those days of arranged marriages, you want to date someone of your own choice.
+ Mendel and Sadie have a difference of opinion on which relative they should name the baby after, or what the name should be.
+ Etc.

Continue to do this exercise as you did in the Warm-Up that focused on modern day conflicts. 1) Each pair finds a special space and freezes in tableau. At a signal from you, they all argue *without* words; *freeze*; and then *with* words. 2) Then each pair (one at a time) convinces and persuades. Remind them that they cannot argue or yell. They must reason and appeal to each other, compromise or solve the problem. Let each pair improvise the conflict, and then have them *freeze*.

Repeat this exercise with a different group of 8-10 students, until every student has participated in this activity.

Some additional ideas: 1) Each group can re-do their conflict and add obstacles: How would they have the same conflict at night when it's quiet, or when they do not want anyone to hear them, or outside on a windy day. 2) Students can reverse roles with their partners. You can also ask the audience to be the wise person and offer solutions to each conflict.

After the conflict improvisations are completed, ask for two students to improvise the end of the scene when Sadie convinces Mendel that he must seek advice from the wise Rebbe (Rabbi).

Note: Each group of 8-10 students should have different conflicts and characters. Remind students of the audience rule: The audience watches and listens. They do not do the thinking or acting for the actors, unless asked to do so.

VOCAL Track 20 Track 21

Not only do these characters have conflicts in their crowded house, but they also have conflicts about how to sing! To prepare for this scene vocally, learn "Hinei Ma Tov" (**CD Tracks 20–21**).

First teach it to the students on "lah" and then teach the lyrics being mindful of the pronunciation. When the class has learned the melody and words, tell them they will now sing it in a round just as they sang "Debka Hora" in the Warm-Ups. Remind them to pay attention to their part, and don't be distracted by the other parts.

Notice the translation: *It is so good and pleasant when brothers get together!* Ask the class if this is really the way that the family feels right now? Are they happy they are together? Are they enjoying each other's company?

- Find a partner (it can be the same partner as in the drama scene or a new partner). Be sure everyone knows who their character is (the brother, mother, father, sister, animal, etc). Everyone will need a name—refer to **Drama Scene 1** for name suggestions.

- Each duo will sing the round—but differently. In other words, person #1 likes to sing legato, but person #2 likes to sing staccato; or person #1 likes to sing soft, but person #2 likes to sing loud; person #1 likes to sing with lots of vibrato like an opera singer, but person #2 likes to sing with no vibrato; person #1 likes to sing really high, but person #2 likes to sing really low; person #1 likes to sing the words, but person #2 likes to sing on "lah." The cat wants to meow, but the dog wants to bark! What other conflicts can they think of? When each pair has chosen their singing conflict, scene one is ready to begin. Teacher cues them in so that the round starts off correctly. However, let the round take on its own character as the conflicts come to life.

Hinei Ma Tov

Traditional Israeli

Translation: "It is so good and pleasant when brothers are together."

INSTRUMENTAL Track 22

"Let's Work It Out" (Pop Style)

Creating tension and release in improvised music.

◆ Begin with the Pop Style version of "Let's Work It Out" (**CD Track 22**).

◆ Ask students, "What does it feel like to run a race on a really hot day? What is going through your head as you run your very hardest? Are you thinking you want to win? Are you thinking your legs are aching and it is hard to breathe and you can't wait to stop? Are you thinking you want a cold drink of water when you finish, or maybe just to lay down in the cool shade? This is what tension feels like, and the release is the rewards when you finish. What are other examples of tension and release in your life?" (Getting your homework done so you can watch TV; going through a haunted house and being scared but laughing when it is over; being nervous at a concert with everyone watching you, but feeling so happy when you hear the audience clap loudly at the end of the first song).

◆ Explain that tension and release occurs in music and helps to make it interesting. It is sort of like having a conflict, working it out and seeing that everyone is satisfied. Musicians can work out conflicts in music in a variety of ways. Explain that they are now going to explore some ways to create tension and release in music.

Process for both Pop and Klezmer styles

+ Listen to the recording of just the bass and xylphone part then practice the rhythm on pats with left hand on the outside of left thigh and right hand on the inside of right thigh, moving to center of both left and right thighs as the pattern repeats. This will help the students learn to change notes on the instruments. Continue until students have mastered the ostinato.

+ Listen to the recording of the soprano and alto xylophone part then practice with pats similar to above by noticing the rhythm is a little different than the bass xylophone.

+ Prepare glockenspiels by removing low C and D and high F, G and A.

+ Air stick the descending glockenspiel pattern E, E, D, C, C, B, A, A, G, F, F, E. If you have a mallet visual it would help for you to model this part with the students so they can see you change pitches. Say names of notes with air sticking. Xylophone and metallophone players should do this too.

+ Transfer glockenspiel players to instruments and have them play it on the instruments. Xylophones and metallophones should play the part with them.

+ Now add the ostinato parts. Have the ostinato play two patterns (4 measures) before adding the glockenspiel part.

+ Stop the class after they have played for a while. Ask what is creating tension in the music. The students should identify that the xylophones are so loud that they can't hear the glockspiel part. They might also say that the ostinato part is boring or too repetitious. To create some release, what could be done to the music without changing the notes? Experiment with ideas (ostinato plays softer; only a few instruments play ostinato; ostinato plays loud when glocks aren't playing and soft when they are; etc.) There are many solutions, and the class should explore them and then decide which ones they think are the most interesting.

+ Let's create a new source of tension. Ask the glockenspiels to change their F's with F♯ and B's with B♭'s. Now play the piece again and see what is the source of musical tension. Students should identify that the notes don't sound as good together. Explain that the glocks are playing F♯ and B♭ now and the other instruments have B-natural and F-natural on their instruments. Isolate the sound by having everyone play whatever F they have on their instrument together (students might groan) and now try it with the B's. The notes are creating the tension. What would be a solution for a release? Try the ostinato with F's and B's with the glockenspiel part and see if that fixes it.

+ Discuss which ostinatos they prefer, with or without the F♯'s and B♭'s? Adding the F♯ and B♭ brought us closer to the adapted Klezmer mode. Ask the students if they remember what note we need to leave out of the Klezmer mode? (E) The instruments with E's should play D instead. Refer to instrumental Warm-Up #1.

+ Discuss other ways to create tension and release in music and try out ideas. Also talk about how the changed notes created two different styles of music, the pop style harmony and the Klezmer style harmony. "Which style is more interesting to you and why? Does one style seem to create more tension than the other? Why or why not?"

Let's Work It Out

Tension & Release: Pop Style

Kimberly McCord

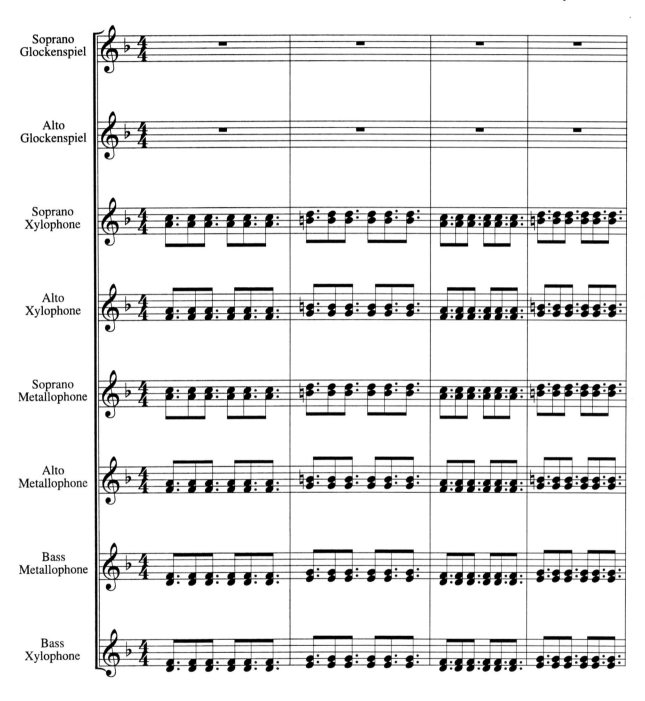

TOGETHER WE CAN IMPROVISE Grades 4–6

TOGETHER WE CAN IMPROVISE Grades 4–6

Let's Work It Out

Tension & Release: Klezmer Style

Kimberly McCord

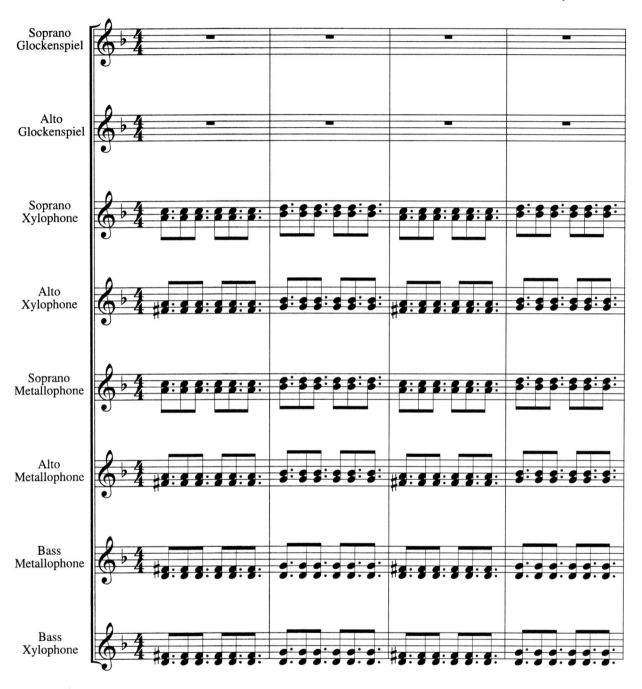

TOGETHER WE CAN IMPROVISE Grades 4–6

SCENE TWO

On his way to the Rebbe, Mendel meets people who live in the town. Brainstorm with the class the type of people who live in a village like this. What shops are there? Occupations? (butcher, baker, yente (gossip), tailor, shoemaker, challah maker, rag seller, bagel maker, peddler, wood chopper, scholar, bricklayer, goat seller, braggart, kvetch (complainer), snob, recluse, bully, the town artist/poet/storyteller, skeptic, adventurous person, argumentative person, etc.).

DRAMA

Ask for 8-10 volunteers to role-play the characters in the village. As Mendel approaches each one, the character will ask him where he is going in such a hurry, and he will explain his problem to each one. Each person will offer advice based on his or her character.

For example:

+ What kind of advice would a happy, friendly six-year old offer? "Here's a lollipop. It will make you feel better," or "Ask my mommy. She always makes me feel better," or "Come to my Bubbe's (grandma), and she'll make you strudel that will make you feel better," etc.

+ What advice would the town pessimist offer? "Don't waste your time. It's useless. Nothing will help," etc.

+ What advice would the optimist offer? "Don't give up. It will all work out. Don't worry, the Rebbe will help you," etc.

+ What advice would the kvetch offer? Does she complain to him and try to top his complaints with her own? "You think you got problems? Mine are worse," etc.

Note: You can have another group of students improvise this same scene with different characters, or have the next group of students play these same characters on Mendel's way home.

★ It is helpful if before you work on this scene, the librarian or classroom teacher works with the class on what types of stores and characters one would find in this type of a village.

VOCAL Track 24

Mendel is always singing (and so are his children and wife, cousins, animals, etc.). As he makes his way through the village he asks people where this wise Rebbe is. Mendel doesn't communicate with words, yet everyone knows exactly what he is asking. It's in his voice and in his movements. Teach "Shalom, My Friends" to the class (**CD Track 24**). Sing it on "lah."

Mendel sings the first four measures to the people that he meets in the village. They, in turn, answer back the last four measures. Before they begin, discuss how Mendel's voice might sound. Is it inquisitive? Impatient? Now, ask the class about the different types of people Mendel might meet in the village and how they might answer his question. Remember, there are no words, only "lah." Encourage the singers to change the consonants and vowels to fit the emotion just as they did for Vocal Warm-Up #3. For example, "heh," "weh," or "zee" instead of "lah." Remind the class that dynamics, tempo and tone make a big difference when we are communicating with the voice. Perhaps Mendel asks a young six-year old girl where the wise Rebbe is. Next he meets an eighty-year old man. Then he meets a group of boys. How do these voices differ? What does a group sound like compared to an individual?

Practice as a class and then ask for volunteers.

Decide who will be which character, and decide how each character will answer Mendel's question.

Shalom, My Friends

Traditional Hebrew

INSTRUMENTAL

Adapted Klezmer mode improvisations

Using the Klezmer mode notes (C, D, F♯, G, A, B♭, C), create improvisations to accompany the characters in the village. Improvisations can be played on recorders, Orff instruments or other instruments capable of using the prescribed Klezmer notes. Try to create an expressive mood to accompany the mood of the character. The improvisation should complement the character but never overpower it.

ADAPTED KLEZMER MODE

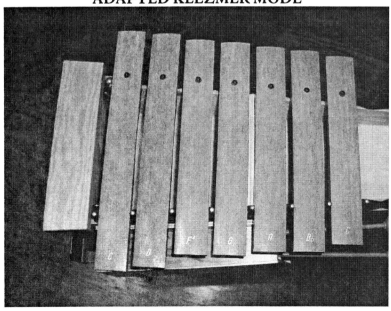

SCENE THREE

Mendel seeks advice from the wise one, explain to the class, the Rebbe. Engage the class in a discussion about a wise person. Consider: How does someone acquire the status of a wise person? What attributes do they look for in a person when they seek advice? Are there different wise people for different problems?

DRAMA

+ Before Mendel arrives at the Rebbe's place, focus on the character of the Rebbe. Let a student role-play the Rebbe in his study as he thinks aloud about people's problems in his village, and what advice he can offer, or how he can help them.

+ Ask for two volunteers to improvise the following scene: Mendel arrives at the Rebbe's study and explains his problem. The Rebbe contemplates the solution, and asks the poor man if he has any animals. Mendel replies that he does have some chickens, a rooster, a goose, a goat and a cow. The Rebbe tells him to go home and bring the chickens, goose and rooster into his hut. Have Mendel react when he hears the advice. Remember, he has to show respect to the Rebbe since he did go to him for advice, and the Rebbe's solutions usually work!

+ Select another volunteer to be Mendel who speaks aloud as he returns home. What is he thinking? How does he think his wife will respond? How will the kids respond? His mother? The animals? What does he think will happen? How will he break the news to them? Does he practice what he's going to say to his wife and family? What will he tell the people in town who know he went for advice? They're probably waiting to hear the Rebbe's solution! Perhaps he meets one of his friends, and practices with his friend what he will say to his family.

★ You can focus on his walk home with the above suggestions without the characters in town, or Mendel can meet them and improvise his answers (or avoidance of answers).

VOCAL Track 20

+ To prepare the class for Mendel's meeting with the Rebbe, review the melody of "Hinei Ma Tov" (**CD Track 20**). Sing it on "lah."

+ Practice singing with the new words. See written music.

+ When Mendel finds the Rebbe, he communicates by singing to him. The Rebbe answers him (see music) in song. This singing exchange is an altered version of "Hinei Ma Tov." Choose volunteers to be the Rebbe and Mendel or divide the class in two, with one half being Mendel and the other half being the Rebbe. Do not sing yet.

+ Think about what Mendel's voice will sound like. Will it be tired? Will it be urgent? Pleading? Crying? Soft? Loud? High? Low? With a vibrato? And how will the Rebbe's voice sound? What does a wise voice sound like? Is it calming? Authoritative? Loud? With a vibrato? Engage the class in a discussion about how these two characters and their voices might differ.

♦ After the class has decided on distinctive voices for Mendel and the Rebbe, begin the singing conversation.

Hinei Ma Tov  Track 25

Traditional Israeli
Original lyrics by Louise Rogers

What can I do Reb-be? Help me. I can-not live in my house.
Ev - 'ry-one yel-ling and sing - ing. Please make my house less crow - ded.

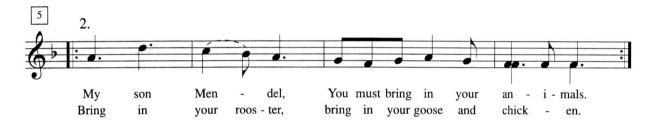

My son Men - del, You must bring in your an - i - mals.
Bring in your roos - ter, bring in your goose and chick - en.

INSTRUMENTAL

Finding Your Personal Style

Locate or download a copy of the recording of "Nigun Tantz" from the recording, *The World of Authentic Jewish Music Poetry.*

★ "Nigun Tantz" means Nigun Dance. A Nigun is a song without words.

♦ Explain that in this recording, they will hear authentic Klezmer music. The main instrument that improvises is the clarinet. This clarinet player is telling a story and representing at least two different moods. Instruct them to listen to the first part of this recording and see if they can identify the two different moods they hear. What might the soloist be saying through music? How does he create a personal style to help represent the mood of the music? Have they ever heard a clarinet played this way? This is actually a very typical sounding clarinet in Klezmer music. The clarinet player slides into notes to create expression. Tell them they can sort of do that on their recorder by covering the holes half-way so they sound a little out-of-tune.

♦ Allow students to experiment with this sound on recorders.

- Explain that improvisers use that sliding sound in their voices or on instruments to create expression. You hear this all the time in blues, jazz, popular music, and rap, just to name a few. It is harder to create that sound on the Orff instruments, but can slide into notes by dragging your mallet from the bar just next to the bar you want to play. If you were playing a B♭ then you can slide up into the B♭ by softly playing the A and sliding up to the B♭, or slide down from the C to the B♭. It works best with metallophones.

- Tell them that musicians work very hard to develop their own personal style. Musicians who are especially original can be identified easily. Other musicians like to copy their style. For example, some clarinet player many years ago probably started playing Klezmer music, and other clarinet players thought it sounded so great they started playing the same way. Pretty soon that one clarinet player's style became the way to play Klezmer clarinet. It is amazing how one person can have such a big influence.

- Ask your students if they have an instrument they especially like to play and why. Is it because of the sound, the way it feels in their hands, or the look of it? What is it about that instrument that they really like? Explain that as they get better and better on the instrument, they will start to find their own way to play the instrument, and when they improvise, those little special ideas of theirs will come out. Tell them that since there have never been any great recorder or Orff instrument playing Klezmer musicians, this is their chance to develop their own style. Imagine kids all over the world wanting to play the recorder or Orff instruments just like you! You invented a style! What would it sound like? Let's continue to develop our Klezmer style.

SCENE FOUR

As Mendel is approaching the house, everyone is busy preparing for either Sabbath or a holiday. (The class can decide on the occasion.)

DRAMA

- Each student is to decide on an action to pantomime (polish candlesticks, make chicken soup, peel onions, dice carrots, peel and grate potatoes, mend a tablecloth, set the table, etc.) Refer to the Warm-Up activities and remind them to include details and think about how they feel.

- At some point during their pantomime, have them begin to show anxiety or concern as they eagerly await Mendel with the Rebbe's solution. Have them *freeze* in a tableau entitled "Anticipation." Then point to each student, and one at a time let each one improvise dialogue.

- Mendel arrives and Sadie steps outside. The group *freezes*.

- Select two students to improvise the scene between Sadie and Mendel. What does he tell her? How does he break the news to her? What is her reaction? Of course Mendel is determined to follow the Rebbe's advise and shoos in the chickens and rooster and goose. You can interview the animals and see how they feel about this solution!

- Have the class create a new tableau entitled "Shocked," as the family watches in disbelief as the animals are brought into the noisy and crowded house. *Freeze*. Now the title changes to "Horror." *Freeze*.

- Conclude the scene with the students doing their chores in pantomime but with the animals clucking and flying and presenting obstacles. At some point, have them *freeze* and create a new tableau, "Chaos," and then, one at a time, when you point to each one, they speak their thoughts aloud, and *freeze*.

- Students can create additional titles for tableaux.

VOCAL Track 17 Track 26

- To prepare for this scene, teach the class "Lo Yisa Goy" (p. 86). Sing this on "lah." After the class is comfortable with the melody, have them sing it in a round. Note the #2 at the 2nd ending. This is where the second voice comes in.

- Review "Debka Hora" (**CD Track 17**) as well from Vocal Warm-Up #2.

- Back at the house, everyone is dancing and clapping the "Debka Hora." Set the scene by having volunteers be the family and friends inside the house. Then ask for two more volunteers to be Sadie and Mendel. Do not begin yet!

- Mendel must tell Sadie what the wise Rebbe has advised. He brings her outside so that he can tell her. As is the case in all of the vocal scenes, Mendel only sings—he does not speak. She must understand what he is telling her by the sound of his voice and his actions. Likewise, Sadie only sings and Mendel must understand what she is telling him through the tone of her voice and her actions.

- Begin the scene by starting the "Debka Hora" inside the house. The scene is loud and fun and everyone is singing the round, clapping and tapping their feet. Two people can go into the middle of the circle and dance. They come out and two more go in. All the while everyone is singing "Debka Hora" in round.

- Now, with the "Debka Hora" going on, Mendel returns to the house and motions to his wife to go outside with him. He must tell her about the wise Rebbe. He knows she will not be pleased with his advice. He dreads having to tell her.

- *Freeze* "Debka Hora" people.

- Mendel sings the melody of "Lo Yisa Goy" (**CD Track 26**) to tell Sadie. Mendel starts the round and Sadie enters at the #2. Remind the class that they must sing in character. What does Mendel have to tell his wife? How does he feel? How does that show in his voice? And what about his wife? How does she feel about this advice? As they sing this round, encourage the singers to be animated and use facial expressions to help get their point across.

Lo Yisa Goy

Traditional Israeli

INSTRUMENTAL

Free Improvisation or Chaos?

Ask the students, "What would a house full of animals sound like? Since animals don't usually perform structured songs, what they do is improvisation. They cluck or oink or make their animal sounds when they want to, or in response to being scared or hungry. One thing with animals is they don't constantly make sounds. They stop and start. They are silent and listen sometimes. In music this resembles a type of style called free improvisation. There are no songs to be learned. You improvise and respond to other people and see what happens. The tricky thing is how to start and stop. A group has to really be paying attention and work together to make it work well. You might all end together or fade out or one person plays the last note. The fun part is you can't predict what will happen; you just go with the flow of things and see what turns out."

Teacher Directions:

+ Divide the class into groups of four or five. Let students choose recorders or Orff instruments and set up in the Klezmer adapted mode (C, D, F♯, G, A, B♭, C).

+ Instruct the students to work on free improvisations based on what the house full of animals might sound like. Each group's improvisation should be a minute or less. There should not be a leader or director. All instruments (animals) should have an equal role.

+ The group should include animals with short sounds and long sounds, high and low, and loud and soft. Let the groups practice doing this for about 10-15 minutes.

+ Ask each group how well they did with no one being a leader and every instrument having an equal role.

+ Have them rate themselves and their group with one finger meaning poor job, two fingers meaning OK job, and three fingers meaning terrific job. Let them know they will get a chance to perform their free improvisations in an upcoming activity.

★ Chaos or kids having fun making music? Be aware that activities like this can feel like out-of-control behavior. Learn to recognize the difference between students engaged and excited about improvising and students with off-task behavior. As a teacher you will be more of a guide, trying to let them create with little interference from you.

It is also a good idea to warn other teachers and administrators that you will be doing this activity ahead of time. It might seem like chaos for someone passing by your room!

SCENE FIVE

Ask the students what they think has happened after three days have passed, and things have become worse. Some ideas: chickens gave birth; feathers are in the soup; chickens peck at homework; animals make holes in sweaters and blankets; the rooster crows at the wrong time; etc.

DRAMA

Divide the class into groups. Allow time for each group to prepare a short scene that depicts life in the crowded hut. Each group will decide *how* they want to present their scene. When the groups are ready, each group will present their scene to the class.

Some suggestions:
- A scripted scene with a beginning, middle and end
- Conversations between people in the house, or people from the house and their friends
- A dream sequence (escape or a nightmare)
- Monologues (a one person speech) from different characters in the house, or readings from diary entries
- Conversations between the animals, or the people and the animals (at least the cow won't talk back!)
- A scene in song only, or through instruments only

Ask for two volunteers to conclude the scene with Sadie telling Mendel he must go back to the Rebbe to tell him that his advice made things worse.

★ As you check each group's ideas, make sure they have a clear sense of who, what, where, and when, and that each one in the group knows the character he or she is portraying.

VOCAL

Things have become worse! At this point, the animals have been brought in, and the little crowded house is even more crowded!

Set the scene with many volunteers singing in duos, trios or quartets. Explain to the class that they can chose from any of the rounds that we have learned so far—except for "Lo Yisa Goy" which is reserved for Mendel and Sadie. Include the animals in this scene. Perhaps the animals are chasing each other around the house as they sing (or cluck!) the round. Are the children marching in a parade? Perhaps they're chasing the animals. Generate a list of activities to chose from and make sure that the characters know their actions.

Remind the students that they must still sing and show their emotion through their voices and actions. Be sure to sing the rounds in the same key (E minor is good). The class can make up words such as "heh," "geh," "tye," "poh," etc. to get the story across as they did in Vocal Warm-Up #3.

Songs to chose from: *Hinei Ma Tov; Shalom, My Friends; Debka Hora*

Conclude this scene with Sadie pulling Mendel aside. This time, Sadie begins the round "Lo Yisa Goy" demanding that Mendel must go back to the Rebbe and tell him that things are worse. Mendel enters the round at the number 2. Remember that Mendel and Sadie must tell the story with their voice and no real words. How do their voices differ from the first time they sang this? Is her voice more demanding? Is the tempo different? More urgent? How does Mendel's voice sound?

INSTRUMENTAL

"It Could Always Be Worse!"

Locate or download a copy of the recording "Der Rebbe Zingt" from *The World of Authentic Jewish Music Poetry*. "Az Der Rebbe Zingt" means When the Rebbe Sings. The translation of the words is as follows:

When the Rebbe sings,

All the Khasidim sing,

And when he dances,

They all dance,

And when he sleeps,

All the Khasidim sleep,

And when he laughs,

They all laugh with him,

When he eats,

They also stuff themselves,

But when he talks,

The Khasidim are quiet.

★ Students generally struggle with triple meter since it is not a familiar meter used in popular music. To familiarize them with triple meter it is best to begin first by feeling the meter through movement, and then they will be more successful on instruments.

Move to the music in order to feel the $\frac{3}{4}$ waltz feel before performing "It Could Always Be Worse!"

Instruct students to take one big step followed by two little steps and to avoid bumping into anything or any person in the room. Tell them to mix in forward movement with side movements.

Teaching Process 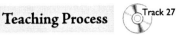 Track 27

+ Bass and contrabass instruments play on count one or the long step from the movement activity. They will play on D only. Bass xylophones can play octave D's, or alternate hands or play just low D. Let them decide what sounds best. Add hand drums on count one too.

+ Teach the other Orff parts by using the first chord patting on left outside and right inside of thigh then moving to center of thighs for the second chord. These instruments will play only on counts two and three. Add tambourine on counts two and three.

+ Using the Klezmer mode (C, D, F♯, G, A, B♭, C) have students work in free improvisation small groups to develop a melody on recorders. The melody should have four phrases and end on a D. It usually helps to repeat a phrase once.

+ The groups should perform their melody with the accompaniment of "It Could Always Be Worse!" (**CD Track 27**). They should select one or two people to play the melody on recorder and or glockenspiels.

+ Perform the melodies for the class. This will likely take one entire class period to do.

+ Improvisations will be added in the next activity.

It Could Always Be Worse!

Kimberly McCord

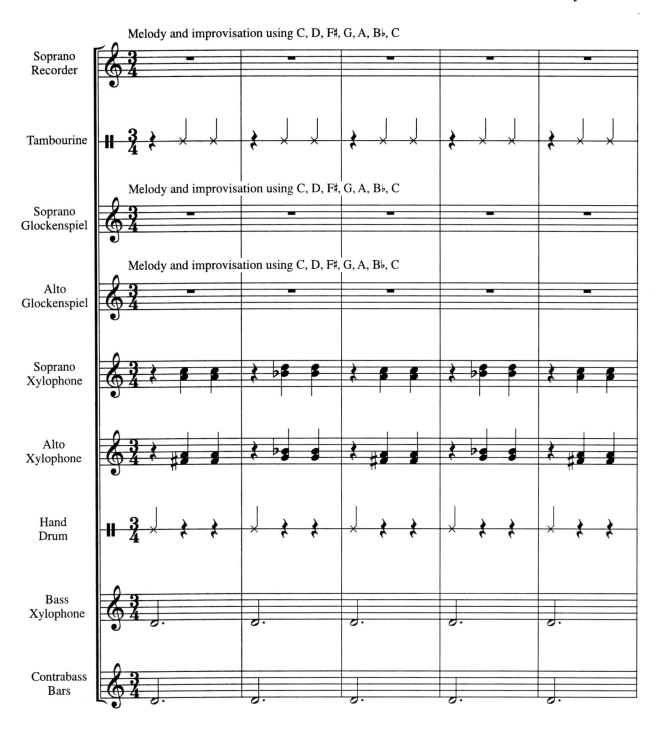

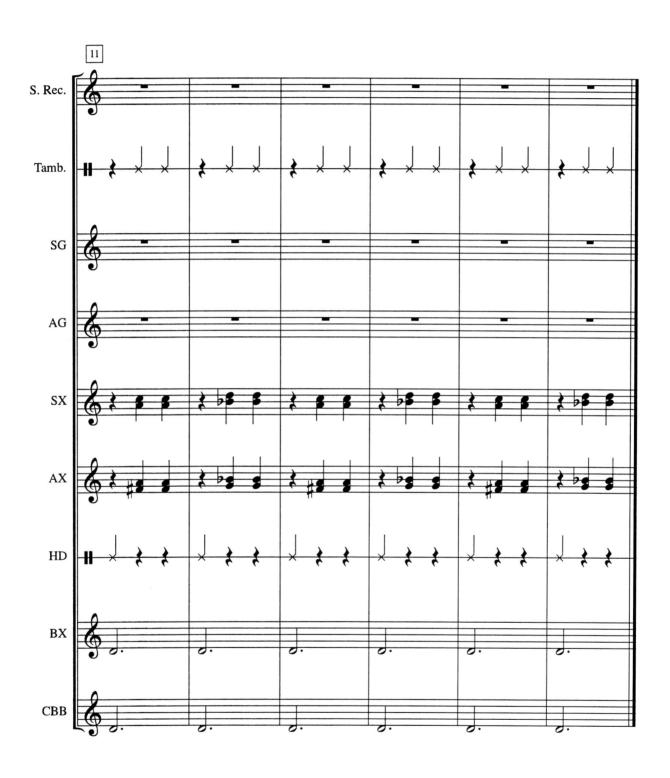

SCENE SIX

Explain to the class that once again, Mendel heads back to the Rebbe.

DRAMA

Recreate the village with new characters, or the same characters as in Scene Two, but different actors.

Some suggestions on how to make this scene different than Scene Two:

+ Add an antagonist...someone who would *like* to be the wise man in the village and who always contradicts the advice the Rebbe gives, because he thinks he is wiser than the Rebbe. He stops Mendel and gives him his advice. Improvise the scene.

+ Add a group of yentes (gossipers) who engage in exaggerated gossip about Mendel's crowded house ("I heard the girls had feathers in their hair at school the other day. Sadie came to the synagogue meeting with egg yolks on her socks. Mendel had a seven-inch hole in his jacket from his chicken's pecks. They can't find one of the children. I saw one of the kids sleeping on the roof." etc.). You can also have fun with how different ages gossip. How do seven-year olds gossip? Seventeen-year olds? Seventy-one-year olds? Does Mendel see them and try to avoid them or confront them?

+ Ask the class what else could happen on the way to the Rebbe? Solicit ideas and improvise the ideas.

At some point, shift the focus to the house. Someone in town has decided to write a story about the members of the household. You (or a student) can be the interviewer. The interviewer calls one family member at a time out of the house for the interview. The class can generate a list of interview questions. Suggestions:

+ Please describe how you feel, using a metaphor or a simile.

+ If you could escape from here, where would you go?

+ What do you think the solution to the problem is, and how can you accomplish that?

VOCAL ⊙ Track 24

Ask for volunteers to be Mendel, the villagers and the Rebbe. Decide who the villagers will be and if they will be different than they were in Scene Two.

So, once again, Mendel walks to the village to get advice from the wise Rebbe. He searches for the Rebbe but he is nowhere to be found. He asks some of the local villagers where the Rebbe is. He asks by singing "Shalom, My Friends" (**CD Track 24**) in the same way that it was done in Vocal Scene Two. They answer him in song, but they do not know where the Rebbe is. Where could he be? Mendel starts to call for him in desperation. He cups his hands around his mouth and in a loud, strong voice he begins to sing "Shalom, My Friends" (on "lah") right in the middle of the village!

Ask the class to sing this in their strongest, clearest voice. Ask them if they have ever called out to their dog to come home for dinner, or yelled for their mom or dad at a soccer game, etc. Use that voice! Mendel really wants to find the Rebbe! Now, ask for volunteers to sing alone or with partners.

Suddenly, he hears a very wise voice in the distance; the Rebbe's voice. The Rebbe sings the round with Mendel (entering at the pick up to measure 5). Mendel follows the sound of his voice until he finds the Rebbe.

SCENE SEVEN

Mendel arrives at the Rebbe's study and explains that things are worse because now, in addition to the lack of space and arguments, there's clucking, honking, crowing, pulling, shoving, and no one can move, breathe, eat or sleep. The Rebbe listens and asks him if he has any other animals. He replies he has a cow and a goat. The Rebbe advises him to bring both of them into the house.

DRAMA

Select two students to improvise this scene, and focus on Mendel's reactions!

VOCAL

Similar to Vocal Scene 3, Mendel and the Rebbe have a singing conversation. Discuss with the class how the wise Rebbe's voice differs from Mendel's at this point. Does the Rebbe's voice sound any different than it did the first time they met? Is he still calm and wise? Is Mendel's voice different now that he is living in a house that is even worse than it was? Is Mendel angry at the Rebbe? Confused?

After Mendel sings his problems to the Rebbe, much to Mendel's disappointment, the Rebbe once again delivers some confusing advice. He tells him to bring in the rest of his animals.

Ask the class to come up with their own ending to the song. Their lyrics should reflect the Rebbe's advice.

SCENE EIGHT

Mendel returns home.

DRAMA

+ Ask for two volunteers to improvise Mendel's thoughts as he walks home. Does he try to avoid everyone who is eager to hear the Rebbe's advice? Does the antagonist who disagrees with the Rebbe's advice confront him?

+ You can keep this scene simple, repeat the village scenes from earlier in the story, or elicit new ideas from the class.

VOCAL Track 24

Mendel leaves the village waving goodbye to the village folk. As he leaves he sings "Shalom, My Friends" (**CD Track 24**). However, as he tries to leave the village, people stop him to ask what the Rebbe has advised this time. He is worried about getting home and delivering this news to Sadie and the rest of the family. He tries to be polite as he encounters these obstacles and concentrates hard on the task at hand–singing goodbye and getting home! Ask for volunteers to be the villagers and for one to be Mendel.

Discuss with the class possible ways that Mendel could be interrupted by the curious village folk. Refer to the list of obstacles or interruptions that the class generated in Vocal Warm-Up #4 and then create a new list for this scene. Remind the class that Mendel must remain singing "Shalom, My Friends" even if as he encounters these obstacles and is repeatedly interrupted.

INSTRUMENTAL Track 27

"It Could Always Be Worse!" (CD Track 27)

+ Using the Klezmer mode (C, D, F♯, G, A, B♭, C), choose two people to improvise Mendel's thoughts with the antagonist. Use the "It Could Always Be Worse!" accompaniment.

+ On the recording you will hear one soloist playing recorder and another playing glockenspiel. Select two new soloists and continue to discuss how closely the improvisations mirrored the drama.

SCENE NINE

The family awaits Mendel and the Rebbe's solution.

DRAMA

- Have the students select partners and conflicts. Start with a tableau, and then bring the tableau to life. In the middle of the conflicts, Mendel returns and pushes and pulls the goat and the cow into the house.

- Repeat the sequence from Scenes Four and Five.

Note: You can work the conflicts the same way as you did in Scene One, or you can try one or both of the following:

- Each pair starts the conflict improvisation with "I will/I won't!" or "Please/No!"

- Provide each pair (one pair at a time) with a "first line." As soon as you call out the line, the pair begins the improvisation with the first line you provide. Remind the students that the house is filled with feathers, animal sounds, etc., so that the way they speak and act should take into consideration the chaos and cramped space.

Suggestions for first lines:

My head hurts.

I wish I could get out of this house.

We'll never be able to sleep.

Are you thinking what I'm thinking?

I hate this chore.

Where is my new hair ribbon?

Has anyone seen the baby's rattle?

I have mud on my new shirt.

Now listen carefully. Here's the plan.

What was that noise? or What is that smell?

Do you see what I see?

I'm getting claustrophobic.

Ow! I just got a splinter in my foot.

Who used up the hot water?

How come I did not get a cookie?

I do not want to read to you.

The soup is burning.

Has anyone found Grandma's glasses?

I don't feel good.

I'm really mad.

Help! I'm stuck!

I hope this candle does not burn out.

If I have to tell you one more time.

I told you so.

I'll never trust you again.

You really expect me to believe that?

When will you ever grow up?

Why do things always happen to me?

Where did you get that?

It's not my fault.

VOCAL  Track 26

A Stomping Mad Family!

+ Prepare the class for this scene by clapping "Lo Yisa Goy." Once the class is comfortable clapping the rhythm, have them snap it, pat it, and finally stomp it! Encourage the class for other ways to play the piece rhythmically. They do not sing it, but ask where they can place the beat? On their legs, on their desk? How about some mouth percussion? Can they smack their lips together? Now, divide the class in two and rhythmically perform "Lo Yisa Goy" in a round.

+ Ask for volunteers to be Mendel, Sadie, the various family members and animals. Some animals will be inside the house, and others will be with Mendel.

The Scene

+ Begin the scene with the family and animals inside the house. Suddenly the door opens and Mendel walks in. Accompanying Mendel are all of the other animals.

+ Freeze all activity so that Mendel can sing.

+ Mendel sings "Lo Yisa Goy" (without words) (CD Track 26) explaining that he is only following the advice of the wise Rebbe.

+ The family and animals are so angry at this horrible advice that they stomp, clap and beat their part! There are no words to describe how they feel as they rhythmically pound their part of the round. Remind the students that it is still in the form of the round but Mendel is the only one who sings.

INSTRUMENTAL

"It Could Always Be Worse!"

+ Select one of the melodies the groups of students developed in the last lesson. If you have time, notate the melody before the class meets so you can teach the melody to the entire class. Students can choose to play the melodies on recorder or glockenspiels.

+ Create an arrangement of the piece to include free improvisation sections alternating with melody and call and response using tension and release or surprises in improvisations. The free improvisation sections will even include students playing instruments other than recorder and glockenspiel. Decide how to start and end the piece. Perhaps select a conductor to help cue in the sections.

SCENE TEN

Mendel arrives at the Rebbe's study and tells him that things can't possibly get worse. The Rebbe tells him to go home and let all the animals out of the house. Mendel is not sure he heard him correctly, so he repeats the instructions. He wonders why he should take the animals out if he told him to bring them in.

DRAMA

+ Ask for a volunteer to be Mendel as he returns to the Rebbe. He can speak his thoughts aloud. He can meet characters who repeat some of the yente's exaggerated rumors (the goat's wearing grandma's wig; the front door is blocked; someone threw a chicken egg thinking it was a ball and it is dripping down the eldest sister's wedding dress; will there even be a wedding? etc.). The yentes can incorporate the five senses into their gossip (It smells like…sounds like….etc.)

+ Ask for two volunteers to role-play Mendel, who tells the Rebbe how horrible the situation is, and the Rebbe, who advises him to remove all the animals. Challenge the actor to capture Mendel's exasperation and frustration as he tells the Rebbe how horrible the situation is, and then his reaction when he is told to take all the animals out of the hut.

+ Elicit ideas from the class for Mendel's trip home. Does he try to figure out a way to get home without seeing anyone? Improvise their ideas.

VOCAL  Track 25

Whispering Advice From the Rebbe

+ To prepare the class for this scene, have them sing "Hinei Ma Tov" (**CD Track 25**) as softly as they can (so softly and calmly that they can sing it in the ear of the person right next to them as if they are telling them a secret).

+ Ask for volunteers to be Mendel and the wise Rebbe, or split the class in two groups assigning one group to be Mendel and the other to be the Rebbe.

+ Set the scene with a very pensive Rebbe sitting by himself. Teacher says "begin" and in walks Mendel who is not very happy! At this point Mendel can't understand how things could get any worse and why the Rebbe has given him such bad advice! He is at the end of his ropes. He sings his song to the Rebbe as he has done many times before. Ask the class how Mendel's voice might sound different this time.

+ The very wise Rebbe motions to Mendel to come close … closer … and closer still so that the Rebbe can whisper sing into Mendel's ear. Have the class, as they have done before, create the Rebbe's lyrics for his ending advice. Remind them that this last and final time he advises Mendel to take all of the animals out of the house. Discuss how the Rebbe's whisper sing might sound. Does he still sound wise?

SCENE ELEVEN

Mendel returns home, and tells the family the Rebbe's solution. They release all the animals and enjoy the freedom of their space. They realize that no matter how bad things are, things can always be worse.

DRAMA

Involve the entire class in this final scene, either as the people in the hut, the hut that is about to split at the seams, the animals, or even some of the inanimate objects such as the kitchen table or the bed.

+ Begin with a tableau of the crowded house. Each student, in a special space, decides on an animate or inanimate character, what the character is doing, and an obstacle. (Is the leg of the chair wobbly and the chair wonders what will happen if Grandma sits on it?)

+ Since the family has no idea what advice the Rebbe has given this time, and no one dares move or speak, have them *freeze* in a tableau entitled "Fear!" Then, as you point to each student, he or she improvises a line of dialogue that expresses his or her feelings.

★ You can also include some pantomime with obstacles as you did in Warm-Up #4. For example: you try to braid hair, but chickens land on your head; you try to mend a dress but can't find your glasses that fell on the floor; a baby chick needs to find its mother; you need to go outside to milk a cow, but keep slipping on an egg that fell on the floor; you must write an important letter, but you have a cut and your finger is bleeding; you're kneading dough and notice feathers in the dough and you have three minutes to get the pie in the oven; etc.

+ While they're posed in the tableau, they hear Mendel shouting as he is running down the road, "Everyone. Open the windows. Open the door. The Rebbe says to let all the animals out of the house. Push them out. Pull them out. No more animals in the house!" The tableau comes to life and everyone, *in pantomime*, helps remove the animals. Challenge them to maintain a special space as they do this, and to focus on details (Do they have to coax the animal to come to them? Do they have to open a window while holding a bird in their hand? Is the cow being stubborn and won't leave? etc.).

+ When all the animals are outside, instruct them to *freeze*, look around them, take a deep breath, feel the freedom of space, and *freeze* as a tableau entitled "Freedom." Then point to each student, and allow time for each student to improvise how he/she feels. This can be done through dialogue (words or song!) and/or movement (whirl, twirl, stretch, etc.).

+ Elicit ideas from the class on how they would like to state the moral, "No matter how bad things are, things can always be worse!" Do they resolve never to complain again?

+ Conclude the story. Have a volunteer be Mendel as he returns to thank the Rebbe for his wise advice. Challenge the student to speak Mendel's thoughts as he passes through the village, and to focus on his feelings. Is he happy? Is he perplexed? Does he move differently than the other times he headed to the Rebbe? What does he say to the Rebbe? Have a student role-play the Rebbe. How does the Rebbe react? Does he speak? If so, what does he say?

Note: You can improvise this scene with just Mendel and the Rebbe, or elicit ideas from the class as to how they would like to improvise this scene. Mendel can meet the philosopher or other characters. Maybe there are some students who did not have an opportunity to role-play a character in the village. This would be an opportunity for them to do so.

VOCAL  Track 25

The Quiet House!

In our final scene, the family is singing the round "Hinei Ma Tov" (**CD Track 25**). Mendel and Sadie sit quietly reading and sipping their tea.

- Lead the class in a discussion of what makes this final scene so different from Vocal Scene 1.

- Read the translation and ask the class if the family feels any different about each other in this scene than they did in the first scene. What makes it different this time?

INSTRUMENTAL Track 27

"It Could Always be Worse!"

Perform "It Could Always Be Worse!" (**CD Track 27**) with free improvisations of the animals leaving the house. This time do not let the groups prepare their free improvisation, but rather, have them perform in the moment. Remind them to listen carefully to each other, make sure no one instrument or animal dominates the improvisation, and to listen for the ending. The improvisations shouldn't last any longer than a minute and should be alternated with the melody or call and response improvisations between two people. The class should develop the arrangement.

CREATIVE EXTENSIONS

- **Multicultural Activity:** Divide the class into groups. Each group will select a country/culture and adapt "It Could Always Be Worse!" to fit the country/culture. Remind them that a folktale reflects the country from which it originated, so although the plot will be the same, they need to consider who the wise man is (chief, shaman, the eldest, etc.), what types of animals, dwellings, occupations, characters, names for characters, conflicts, idioms, etc. Each group will plan their version of the folktale, and then perform it for the class as a play, or tell it as a story. Make sure each group has a different culture/country, so that they see several multicultural versions of the same story.

- Piece together the improvisations and perform the story as a play.

- Perform the story as a play. *Things Can Always Be Worse*, by Lois Kipnis, published by The Dramatic Publishing Company, Woodstock, Illinois, is a play version of the story, with room for improvisation throughout it. You can weave in some of your own improvised scenes.

- Write and perform an original fable using "It Could Always Be Worse!" as the moral.

- Act out the whole story using only pantomime, or using only dance or music, or using only sounds.

- You can add scenes to the story. For example, what if a music group is lost and they stop at the house. Their cart has a broken wheel. One of the children always wanted to be a singer and hopes maybe she could run away with this troupe.

- Select a student or panel of students to be the wise person for the class for one week. This student or students will solve each problem that arises in the class during that week. Hold an election for that position. Have students give campaign speeches and nominating speeches.

- Discuss how a town meeting is run, and have a town meeting to decide what to do about this house that has become a neighborhood annoyance.

Variations of the Folktale or the Theme

- *Could Anything Be Worse?* retold by Marilyn Hirsch

- *Could Be Worse!* by James Stevenson

- *Famous Fables for Little Troupers*, retold by Dr. Greta Lipson (Good Apple Publication)

- *It's Too Noisy* by Joanna Cole

- *Too Much Noise* by Ann McGovern

- *Always Room For One More* by Sorche Nic Leodhas

Play Version

Things Can Always Be Worse by Lois Kipnis (The Dramatic Publishing Company)

SHAKESPEARE'S MACBETH

Objectives

- Students will acquire an appreciation for Shakespeare's language and be able to interpret, improvise and speak lines from *Macbeth*

- Students will collaborate and determine the best ways to dramatize a scene

- Students will develop improvisations into scenes for shared performances

- Students will demonstrate an understanding of the characters they portray by creating appropriate dialogue and using appropriate voices, body movement, and gestures

- Students will stage scenes and determine how to effectively use the stage space

- Students will create sound effects to create a mood, and perform effectively for selected scenes

- Students will evaluate their improvisations, and try alternate ways to develop each improvisation/ scene

- Students will use pantomime and details to create believability

- Students will understand and demonstrate in their improvisations the motives of characters

- Students will perform expressively on instruments

- Students will sing expressively

- Students will speak and move expressively

- Students will develop arrangements of pieces they learn to play or sing

- Students will sing, play instruments, and act alone and in groups

- Students will improvise soliloquies

- Students will read, interpret, and execute stage directions in a play

- Students will read scenes from plays for meaning, and give meaning to the words they speak

- Students will demonstrate an understanding of metaphors and similes

- Students will understand emphasis and inflection

- Students will collaborate to select the most effective ways to create a sense of evil and foreshadowing to set the mood for each scenes

- Students will role-play moral dilemmas

National Standards for Theatre: Standard #1, 2, 3, 4, 6, 7
National Standards for Music: Standard #1, 2, 3, 4, 6, 7, 8, 9

Materials
- Collections of Shakespeare's play, *Macbeth*, as well as story adaptations (bibliography is provided)
- Optional: a large cauldron and large pieces of black fabric
- Boomwhackers, hand drums, recorders, soprano, alto, bass metallophones, soprano, alto, bass xylophones, contra bass bars, soprano and alto glockenspiels, triangle, and chime tree. Some of these instruments can be substituted with boomwhackers, or pieces can be performed without Orff instruments (see specific pieces for ideas)

Prior Knowledge
- Students are familiar with the definition of *improvisation* in music and drama
- Students are familiar with the definition of a *scene* and an *act* in a play
- Students are familiar with the definition of *pantomime*
- Students are familiar with *special space* and *freeze* and *focus*
- Students know how to play various unpitched percussion instruments
- Students know how to play Orff instruments
- Students are familiar with Shakespeare, where he lived, and the time period in which he lived and wrote his plays

INTRODUCTION TO THE UNIT

This unit is set up in a way that you do not need to be an expert on Shakespeare, or trained in theatre in order to engage and motivate your students to read and perform scenes from Shakespeare. We have provided you with improvisational options that range from short exercises to complete scenes. Start at your comfort level. The goal is to make Shakespeare fun and accessible. You do not have to do the entire unit—unless you'd like to! Nor do you have to do it in the sequence we have provided. There are many ways to work with this unit.

- You can work on just one selected Warm-Up, or a scene in the core activities, or as many Warm-Ups and scenes as you want. If you focus on only one scene, we suggest one of the scenes with the witches, as students love to role-play those characters.

- You can complete drama activities only, vocal or instrumental activities only, or a combination of these disciplines.

- You can use the text that we've included in the Core Activities, or you can work in improvisation mode, using the recommended story adaptations of *Macbeth*.

Note: This unit focuses on the performance aspects of the play. If you want to further explore theme, characters, poetic language, irony, etc., we have provided you with suggested resources at the end of the unit. Plot outlines and hand out sheets are also included at the end of the unit.

IMPROVISATIONAL WARM—UPS

TO PREPARE FOR THE PLAY AND GENERATE AN INTEREST IN THE PLAY

- Review *audience rule, freeze* and *focus, improvisation, pantomime, role playing,* and *special space.*

- Explain to the class that in this unit, they will improvise selected scenes from Shakespeare's play, *Macbeth.* As actors, vocalists, and musicians, their challenge will be to give meaning to the words they speak, create believable characters, and set the mood of evil for each scene with sounds and instruments.

WARM—UP #1

DRAMA

- Explain that as they dramatize and role-play characters from *Macbeth*, it is not enough to wear the costume of a witch, or transform faces with makeup into a wicked witch. They must *become* that character in their faces, voices, and bodies. They must think, move, and act as that character. They must give meaning to the words they speak. How they deliver the lines depends on who they are, where they are, what they want, how they feel, as well as other factors.

- Begin each of the following exercises with the class speaking the words and sentences together, and then ask for individual volunteers and ideas.

Exercise #1

Ask the class how they would say *oh* if:
- Someone stepped on their foot.
- They're sleepy.
- They won free tickets to a baseball game.
- A parent says they can't go to the baseball game.
- Someone punched them in the stomach.
- They received a great report card.
- They did not receive a good report card.
- The dentist's drill hit a nerve in a tooth.
- They're eating a cool ice cream on a hot day.
- They taste something they don't like.
- They're in the middle of a computer game and a parent says to shut it off and do homework.
- Their team just scored the winning goal in a soccer game.

Ask for volunteers to add other ways to say *oh*, and ask the class how the person is feeling based on how he or she speaks the word.

Ask the class how they would say *hello* if they're:
- Happy to see someone
- Not happy to see someone
- Surprised
- Being ignored
- Disgusted
- Excited
- Shy
- A super cool dude
- Grumpy
- Phony
- Snobby
- Friendly
- Trying to scare someone
- Evil
- Threatening someone
- etc. (let the class generate ideas)

Exercise #2

- How would they say *I am going* if they're: happy, sad, mad, scared, brave, etc.

- How would they ask, *What time is it?* if they're: impatient, curious, nervous, worried, confused, in a haunted house, in class, in a blizzard, etc.

- How would they say *I will go* if they're: brave, sick, bored, determined to get more information, etc.

Exercise #3

+ Explain to the class that not only does *how* we feel, *who* or *where* we are, or *what* we want change the way we say a word or sentence, but the word or words we *emphasize* in a sentence change the meaning. Have them all say the sentence, *I never said that* with the emphasis on *I*. (Allow time.) Ask them "What does that suggest?" Then have them emphasize *never*. What does that suggest? Now emphasize *said*. What does that suggest (that you *thought* about it but never *said* it, or that you *wrote* or *whispered* it)? Now emphasize *that*. What does that suggest? (I may have broken the vase, but I didn't do *that* act.)

+ Explain that in addition to emphasis, inflection (the way our voice goes up or down) changes the meaning of a sentence. Have them say *hello* with a rising inflection, and then with a falling inflection. Does that change the meaning? Have them say each of the following with rising and falling inflections and discuss the differences in meaning: *Oh; Goodbye; Are you going?*

+ Have the class think of other words and phrases, and discuss how emphasis and inflection change the meaning.

Exercise #4

Have volunteers recite the nursery rhyme, "Humpty Dumpty" as:
+ someone who just heard the news
+ in disbelief
+ the Town Crier
+ the Queen who is furious that he couldn't be fixed
+ a nervous servant afraid to tell the Queen
+ a sad little kid who loved Humpty
+ someone who thinks it's really funny
+ a detective trying to figure out what happened
+ a guard trying to keep curiosity seekers away from the accident scene
+ a king who was jealous of Humpty
+ the court jester (a mime)
+ a very dramatic news reporter
+ a teacher breaking the news to a kindergarten class
+ the Queen trying to break the news to Humpty's mother
+ a police officer trying to maintain order while redirecting traffic
+ a curious child with lots of questions
+ one of the King's men
+ an actor or opera singer who has to tell the audience what has happened
+ the doctor who examined him after the fall
+ an evil witch
+ an opera singer
+ a gossip
+ solicit additional ideas from the class

Exercise #5

Focus now on some of the lines uttered by the witches in *Macbeth*. Have students imagine they've just placed ingredients, such as an eye of a newt or the toe of a frog into a cauldron in order to concoct a magic spell. Their task is to chant and dance around the cauldron in order to make the potion work. The words they speak are "Double, double, toil and trouble, fire burn and cauldron bubble."

- First, have the class speak these lines together with no expression. Then explore different ways to speak these lines: to command the pot to boil; to conjure up evil spirits; to terrorize someone; to warn someone; to predict the future; to create an eerie mood for the play; to tempt someone who is weak to take action. Ask for additional ideas from the class.

- Focus on specific words in "Double, double, toil and trouble, fire burn and cauldron bubble." Have everyone say the word *fire* in a monotone neutral voice. Then have them say the word so it *sounds* like fire. Have them say *burn* in a neutral and monotone voice, and then ask them how they can make the word *sound* like it is burning. Do the same for *bubble*.

- Have students take turns saying one of the following words, first in a neutral voice, and then with meaning: *cool, thunder, soft, happy, mad, munch, serpent, bloody, shriek, foul, foggy, calm, battle, growl, hiss, hard, murder, mewed (meowed), powerful, poisoned, boil, sting, trouble, bold, smear, knock, horror, wicked,* etc.

VOCAL

Vocal inflection can change the way we speak and sing. The voice is very expressive and tells many stories. In *Macbeth*, there are three witches. Each witch has a different way of singing.

Before you begin, teach the song, "Stirring Our Brew," to the class. Add witch laughs and cackles at the end for a witchy effect! Stir the brew with your hands as you sing. (May be used as a music reading activity—not recorded.)

Stirring Our Brew

Traditional

Stir-ring and stir-ring and stir-ring our brew   Oo,_____   Oo_____

★ Witches can be male or female, and song key can be changed to fit the situation.

Witch #1: She has a very high voice with an innocent yet sinister quality.

Sing "Stirring Our Brew" an octave higher than it is written.

Sing as if you are:
+ a little girl who has just lied to her parents about painting on the wall, blaming her younger brother
+ an evil mosquito who just bit an innocently sleeping baby
+ generate a list of similar situations with the class

Witch #2: She has a playfully evil, nasty, nasal voice.

Sing "Stirring Our Brew" as if you are:
+ singing with your fingers holding your nose
+ an angry horn honking in the traffic jam
+ generate a list of similar situations with the class

Witch #3: She has a low voice.

Sing "Stirring Our Brew" as if you are:
+ an evil Eeyore from *Winnie the Pooh*
+ a possessed sloth
+ generate a list of similar situations with class

Ask for volunteers for the three witches. Have all of the witches sing in their given voices at the same time. It is fun to add a movement such as stirring the brew in the imaginary cauldron, or stirring the clouds above into a stormy brew.

Now ask the class to create their own witch voices and describe them in their own words as we did above.

INSTRUMENTAL

Creating a Soundtrack

When movies were new, sound wasn't a part of the movies at all. Movie theaters would hire musicians to play the music to accompany the film. It made the movie more exciting, and since then we like our movies to have music!

There are many resources for silent movies. Encourage students to look up silent movies on the internet. Short clips of scenes from silent movies are perfect for composing short soundtracks.

Go to this website, http://www.youtube.com/watch?v=8mBDQXWflbM and watch this short playful YouTube video of a silent film someone made based on *Star Wars*. The students should watch it and describe how the piano music complements the film.

The music creates a fun mood even though in the movie these are moments of high drama and action. What if the soundtrack for this short clip was changed and the music made more suspenseful?

- We are going to create a short soundtrack for this movie clip.

- Begin by creating a storyboard. Have the students map out the important scenes and what ideas they have for sound effects or music to complement the film.

- Now watch the movie again and time the different scenes. (Turn off the computer sound for this bullet and the following steps.)

- Divide the class into groups to create sound effects/music for the different scenes.

- Each group will need to decide what instruments/vocal sounds or found sounds will be most effective, and begin to compose. Students should find a way to notate their sound effects or music so they can remember how to recreate them when the soundtrack is performed. The notation does not have to be music notation. It can be any sort of symbols the students decide would work.

- Play the video a couple of times so the groups can practice.

- Perform the soundtrack, and film the video with the soundtrack.

★ There are many resources for silent movies. This website has hundreds of short clips of scenes from movies that are perfect for composing short soundtracks. You can select any silent or soundie, but use any scene with no sound. http://www.silentmovies.com

---

WARM-UP #2

DRAMA

- Review the definition of pantomime. If you have not introduced pantomime activities, refer to the introductory chapter for ideas. Define *props* (the objects an actor handles, such as a cauldron or a dagger), and *costumes* (what an actor wears, such as a cape or boots).

- Instruct students to find a special space, and to remain in that special space while they complete the following pantomime exercises.

Pantomime Exercise #1

Have the class imagine they're either an actor or the new Costume and Prop Master for a Shakespearean Theatre Company. It is their first day and they need to check the inventory. Costumes and props are in boxes, locked trunks, or on shelves, etc. Instruct them to take their time as they open each trunk or box, and to really see each thing. They can imagine there is a mirror in front of them, and they can try on costumes and use the props. Focus them on how they handle each object or costume. How would they hold and examine a large brimmed hat with a huge feather? What if it were dusty? How would they try on a heavy velour cape? How would they handle a sword, or put on a jacket or a dress? Consider if it has buttons, hooks, or zippers, etc.

As they pantomime, you can guide them with the following instructions:

+ Look in the mirror and become the character that the costume or prop suggests.

+ Try on different masks and wigs.

+ Feel different fabrics, cobwebs, dust on an old trunk, putty for false noses, etc.

+ Smell the mustiness of costumes or old trunks, a perfumed handkerchief, etc.

+ Hear the rustle of a mouse, the top of a heavy trunk slam shut, sounds from a music box, etc.

+ Struggle with a box that won't open, or lift a heavy box, etc.

+ Take an imaginary piece of fabric, and explore how many things it can become.

Pantomime Exercise #2

+ Have students find a special space and imagine they are the witches in *Macbeth*. Each one has a large imaginary cauldron in front of them. They are in a competition to determine who can concoct the most powerful brew! Have them take out their witches' cookbook, check the ingredients, gather their ingredients, and put them into the cauldron. Challenge them to focus on details (see and feel each ingredient; consider size, texture, smell, etc.).

+ You can state the following before they begin the pantomime, or side coach them as they work. "Is it parsley? Twigs? Worms? Insects? Where do you get the ingredients (thin air, the ground, a secret hole, a pocket?) Do you slice, dice, chew off, or peel each thing? How and with what do you season the brew (salt, pepper, garlic, etc.)? What do you use for liquid (blood, water, oil)? How does it smell? How do you stir it (a ladle, spoon, long fingernail, magic gestures)?"

+ When you feel they have successfully honed their pantomime skills, and the potions are ready, have them do a final stir and taste their concoctions.

VOCAL/INSTRUMENTAL

Sound Brew and Sound Effects

The class will develop a sound track and sound effects to accompany Drama Pantomime Exercise #2 above.

+ Arrange the class into three groups: actors, instrumentalists and vocalists.

+ Teach the bass xylophone part of the piece, "How Weird Are These Sisters?" (p.113). Choose a student to play this part.

How Weird Are These Sisters?

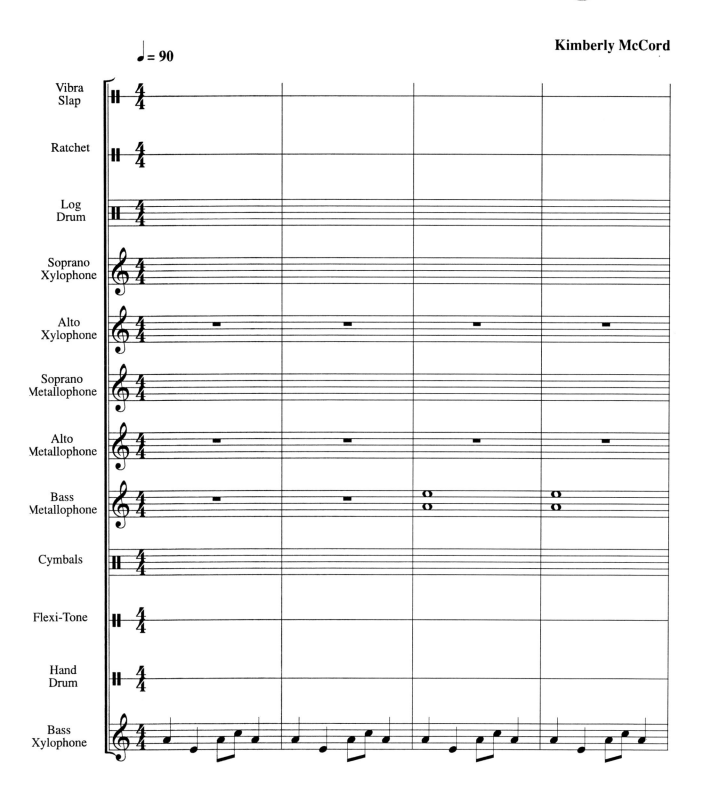

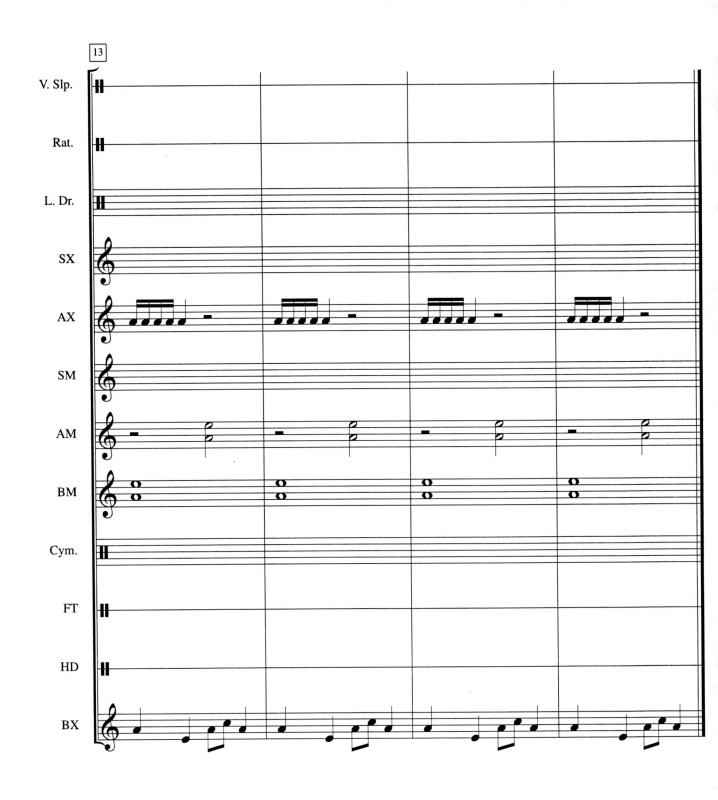

How Weird Are These Sisters?

Compose your own part

Vibraslap

Ratchet

Log Drum

Soprano Xylophone

Cymbals

Flexi-tone

Hand Drum

Other Instrument

Now, choose some instruments that might fit the scene. Consider these questions before you begin:

+ What does it sound like to hit the sides of the cauldron? Is there a clang? What instruments would you use to make this sound?

+ What evil sounds might go into the brew? How can instruments sound evil?

+ Is there an instrument that might sound like each of the witches' voices?

+ What can the voice be used for in this scene? Wind? Bubbling brew?

+ Choose the bass xylophonists, set up the improvisational instruments and be sure the vocalists are clear on their parts and ideas.

Begin the pantomime:

+ Conduct the students as they go, cueing in the different instruments and vocals.

+ Assign a student to be the conductor.

Note: This can also be done in small groups. Each group will perform their scene for their classmates.

WARM-UP #3

Explain that Shakespeare uses asides and soliloquies in his plays. Many times the characters say one thing to the person or people on stage, but then comment or speak the truth to the audience in an *aside*. In other instances, characters are alone on stage and we hear their inner thoughts as a *soliloquy*. Many of these soliloquies reflect a character's *moral dilemma* (a conflict, problem, or situation where the character does not know what to do or say, and there is no easy solution).

Ask the class if they have ever been in a situation where a friend asks them if they like a new dress, shoes, haircut, or bike, etc., and they really don't like it, but don't want to hurt or insult their friend. What do they do or say? Have they ever been in a situation where they're asked to do or say something and they don't want to, or they know it is wrong to do? What do they do or say? For example, if they saw a friend cheat on a test or take someone's lunch, or break a rule in the cafeteria, and a teacher asks them if they know anything about it, what would they do? Would they stick up for their friend, or answer truthfully? Explain that this is a moral dilemma.

DRAMA

Each group will decide on a situation in which one person is asked a question which he or she does not want to answer truthfully, or is asked to do something that he or she knows is wrong. The person is caught in a moral dilemma. Person A in the group will ask the favor or question. Person B in the group will avoid the truth or agree with the other person. Person C will speak the truth either as an aside or as a soliloquy.

For example:

A: "How was my performance in *Macbeth*? Did you like it? Was I the scariest of the witches?"

B: "It was great. You were the scariest."

C: *As an aside to the audience:* "I could hardly hear her, and she looked like she was making a pot of tasty chicken soup rather than an evil broth."

As a soliloquy, alone on stage: "I should tell her that she really should give up on her dream to be an actress. Every part she plays looks and sounds the same. She uses the same voice, and there is no believability to her actions. What should I do? If I tell her the truth, it will shatter her dreams. She's my best friend. She might even think I am jealous of her because I never get a major role in a play."

Some moral dilemma situations to improvise as asides or soliloquies

+ Your best friend throws a rock, breaks a neighbor's window, and runs away. The owner of the house comes out, sees you leave, and accuses you. What do you do?

+ Your best friend confides in you that she is inviting a certain boy to the end-of-the-year party. You planned to invite the same boy. What do you do?

+ You're tired of being teased by a bully in your class. The final straw is that he stole your homework paper, so you'll receive a zero. He's threatened to harm you if you tell the teacher. What do you do?

+ You recently moved to a new community and made friends with some kids whom you have discovered are troublemakers. You changed your group of friends, but now the other group is spreading rumors about you. What do you do?

+ There's a contest at school for the best all-around athlete (or actor, or other). Your sister or brother wants to win and has just asked you to tell your friends to vote for her or him. You have already convinced people to vote for your best friend. What do you do?

+ You're walking home from school, and you see two bullies hitting a younger student. You approach to help the younger one, but the bullies threaten you. What do you do?

+ A friend wants to cut class. You know it is wrong. What do you do?

+ You borrowed (without permission) something from one of your siblings or parent to wear in order to impress everyone at school. However, you either broke it or stained it with permanent markers. Do you admit to the truth, or do you cover it up? What do you do?

- You're at a friend's house eating dinner and you notice a bug crawling in your dinner. The whole family is eating and enjoying the dinner and complimenting your friend's Mom's cooking. What do you do?

- You do not have enough money to buy something you really want. You notice someone drop a wallet and get into a car and drive away. You pick it up. Should you take money out before you locate the owner? What do you do?

- In Shakespeare's days, all parts were played by males. You are an 11 year old boy, and you have been cast as Lady Macbeth in your school play. It's a great role and you would love to play that part, but everyone is teasing you. What do you do?

- You have an opportunity to be selected as the best athlete and the captain of the team. Lately your performance in games has been poor. Someone has convinced you to take steroids. You know it is illegal, and the wrong thing to do. Is it worth the status of team captain or athlete of the year? Deliver a soliloquy.

- Solicit ideas from the class.

Some ideas for soliloquies for moral dilemmas specifically related to the themes in *Macbeth*

- You just finished talking to your best friend who is excited about her superb audition for the lead role in the school play, especially since an agent will be in the audience looking for talent for a television pilot. The phone rings and it is another friend who has an uncanny sense of the future. Whenever she tells you a dream she has had, it comes true. She informs you that she had a dream that you received the lead role in the play, and in her dream she saw your name in lights on Broadway. You finish your conversation with her and wonder if you should try out for the role your other friend wants. Deliver a soliloquy.

- You're in a restaurant and have opened a fortune cookie. It says that you will win the debate, oratory, or storytelling contest and receive fame and money. You had not planned on entering the contest because your sister or brother has been working on a story (or speech) for weeks. The prediction of fame and fortune is tempting. You begin to think of what to do for the contest. Should you enter the contest? Deliver a soliloquy.

- Lady Macbeth sets Macbeth on the path to murder by playing on his cowardice. Imagine you're walking home from a rehearsal and it's dark. Your friend wants to take a short cut through a dark alley. You don't want to. You're afraid. You've heard that the bullies who have been harassing you hang out there. If you say *no*, your friend will call you a coward. Deliver a soliloquy.

VOCAL/INSTRUMENTAL

Familiarize the students with the concept of moral dilemmas, asides and soliloquies. In this Warm-Up, we will explore the idea of how instruments can speak, and how they might deliver the soliloquy or aside.

Musical Elements for Delivering a Musical Soliloquy and Aside:
- Choice of instruments–Which instruments are best suited for the soliloquy or aside?
- Melodically interesting–Be as expressive and interesting as you are when you speak.
- Rhythmically interesting–There are many different rhythms to explore.
- Use of dynamics–loud, soft, crescendos, decrescendos, subito.
- Phrasing–Play as if you are speaking. Where are the pauses?
- Structure–Be organized when you play. Don't play non-sensical!
- Improvisation–After you have established some structure, have fun with some improvisation on the instrument.

Example #1

Soliloquy

You suspect your friend is guilty of some act that broke the law or injured someone. Another friend says he or she has proof of your friend's guilt. You notice that your friend has been acting strangely, so you're beginning to think he or she is guilty.

- Select one student to be the person who delivers the soliloquy. First, decide what would be said with words. Now, ask the student to select instruments and deliver the same scene/soliloquy but with no voice and only the chosen instruments.

Example #2

Asides

A: "How was my performance in *Macbeth?* Did you like it? Was I the best and scariest of the witches?"

B: "It was great. You were the scariest."

C: As an aside to the audience: "I could hardly hear her, and she looked like she was making a pot of tasty chicken soup rather than an evil broth."

- Select a student to deliver the aside (first with words and then with instruments.) He or she may choose to use two instruments: one to speak the sweet lies, "It was great. You were the scariest," and another one that delivers the aside, "I could hardly hear her, and she looked like she was making a pot of tasty chicken soup rather than an evil broth." Before you begin, ask the class which instruments might sound like the sweet lies, and which instruments might sound like the truth.

- Once the students have the hang of this idea, choose more dilemmas. They must do it without speaking first. Instruct the students to mentally formulate what they would say, and then present it with only the instruments.

WARM-UP #4

Explain to the class that when they read a play, there is dialogue (the words the actors speak), and there are stage directions (the words in italics or parentheses that suggest to the actor how to speak the lines, where to move, or what to do). A stage direction might be (*in a whisper*), (*loudly*), (*enter*), or (*hide the dagger*). Explain that the name of the character (or characters) who speaks the line, appears at the beginning of the dialogue. For example:

First Witch: "When shall we three meet again?"

DRAMA

Ask for a volunteer to demonstrate how to speak the line, "Good morning," if the stage direction is *in a whisper*. How will he or she act and deliver the line if the stage direction is *loudly*? If the stage direction is *rushing out the door* or *sit on the throne*?

Have students volunteer to speak the following lines and act out the stage directions.
Note: Some will require more than one student. Read and discuss all of them, and then determine how many students will be needed for each one.

+ **Banquo:** "Who's there?" (*Macbeth enters, accompanied by his Servant carrying a torch*)

+ **Witches:** "Hover through the fog and filthy air." (*exit*)

+ **Macbeth:** "Speak, I charge you." (*Witches vanish*)

+ (*Enter Lady Macbeth, alone, reading a letter*) "They met me in the day of success..."

+ (*The Murderers attack Banquo.*) **Banquo:** (to his son, Fleance) "O treachery! Fly, good Fleance, fly, fly, fly. Thou may'st revenge..." (*Banquo dies. Fleance escapes*)

+ (*Enter the Ghost of Banquo and sits in Macbeth's place*)

+ **Ross** (to Macbeth): "Please't your Highness to grace us with your royal company?"

+ **Macbeth:** "The table's full."

+ **Lennox:** "Here is a place reserved, sir."

+ **Macbeth:** "Where?"

+ **Lennox:** (*pointing to where the ghost sits*) "Here, my good lord."

+ **Witch #1:** "That this great king may kindly say, our duties did his welcome pay." (*Music. The witches dance, and vanish.*)

VOCAL/INSTRUMENTAL

Musical Stage Directions–Sound effects

Sound effects are an important part of live theater. These sound effects can be made with the voice or instruments, and can range from the buzz of an insect to the sound of thunder; from a door creaking to being slammed shut; from a knock on the door to a telephone ringing or a doorbell; from a person snoring to crowds of people laughing.

Generate a list of sounds as possible sound effects. How could these sounds be made? With the voice? The body? The instruments? A combination?

Separate the class into groups and instruct them to write a very short story. It should be the length of a paragraph. The story must have sound effects and these sound effects must be marked.
Before you begin, consider the following questions:

+ Where would they add sound effects?

+ What instruments would they use?

+ Will they use the voice for anything?

+ How will they remember what they played, or will it be different every time?

Ask each group to present their short story with sound effects. They will need either a narrator or actors to present.

WARM-UP #5

Explain to the class that some of the themes in *Macbeth* are ambition, power, greed, evil, murder, the supernatural, hatred, revenge, guilt, confusion, and good versus evil. Many of the characters exhibit these traits, or combinations of these traits. As actors and musicians they will have to figure out how to convey these themes and traits as they improvise scenes.

DRAMA

Character Exercise #1

+ Have students find a special space. Explain that you are a sculptor, and they will be statues with different titles. Each time when you call out a new title, they will slowly transform and become the statue. Tell them that as a sculptor, you take pride in your finished artwork, and like it to be as realistic as possible. They need to transform into statues from the tops of their heads to the tips of their toes. Begin with a statue entitled *Evil*. Have them *freeze*, and then become a statue entitled *Power*. Freeze. Continue with the following titles and others of your choice related to the characters and themes: *confusion, wicked witches, guilt, bravery, jealousy, warrior, fortune-teller, coward, revenge, greed, hatred, ghost,* etc.

+ Now have them become statues of Macbeth, and capture the changes in his character. "Begin as a statue of Macbeth as a brave warrior and a good man. *Freeze.* Slowly transform into Macbeth, the fearful and confused man. *Freeze.* Transform into Macbeth, the ambitious, evil, murdering, revengeful man. *Freeze.* Transform into Macbeth, the defeated man. *Freeze.*"

★ You can also do this exercise using a tableau technique. Divide the class into groups of four to six students. Have each group find an illustration from the play, or a story adaptation of the play, freeze as the photo, and then slowly come to life and speak the thoughts and act out the action suggested in the photos. Bruce Coville's story version of *Macbeth* has some great illustrations, especially of the Weird Sisters.

Character exercise #2

Explain to the class that there is an acting exercise that actors sometimes use for characterization. They decide on an animal image that would be suitable for their character.

+ Ask for four to six volunteers to imagine they're the evil witches in *Macbeth* gathering ingredients for a powerful potion. Have them demonstrate how they would gather and place ingredients in the cauldron if the witches moved and acted as squirrels. Suggest that they start as a squirrel, and then slowly become the witch and keep some characteristics of the squirrel.

+ When the group completes the task, have them become audience members, and ask for another group of volunteers to do the same exercise but with a different animal image. Continue until all students have experienced this exercise. Suggestions: hyenas, giraffes, lions, snakes, foxes, tigers, vultures, fish, kangaroos, etc.

+ After the exercise, discuss whether or not the animal images helped them develop and convey character.

VOCAL/INSTRUMENTAL

Themes and Variations

Divide the class into two groups: instrumentalists and vocalists. Tell the class that they will each have a turn at the instruments as well as singing. It does not matter what instrument they choose. Discuss the following themes and characters with the class. If necessary, provide them with a visual of this list.

Macbeth characters and themes: ambition, power, greed, evil, murder, the supernatural, hatred, revenge, guilt, confusion, good versus evil, confusion, guilt, bravery, jealousy, warrior, fortune-teller, coward, and revenge plotter.

Before you begin, explain to the class that instrumentalists will improvise a *Macbeth* theme melody, and vocalists will answer with a melody which suggests the opposite of the Macbeth melody in some way.

Consider these questions:

+ What would ambition sound like played on an instrument? Strong or weak?

+ What would the voice sound like if it had no ambition at all? Loud or soft?

+ What would *good* sound like on an instrument?

+ What would an evil voice sound like?

Instruct the class to choose partners and practice on their own. After ample time, ask each pair to take turns presenting their theme and variation to the class.

WARM-UP #6

Explain that many of Shakespeare's plays include insults. We suggest that you use your judgment as to whether or not to do this activity depending on your class, and how they will handle this activity during and after class. If you do engage the class in this activity, we suggest you keep the exercise short and fast moving. It is a fun way for students to speak some of Shakespeare's words.

DRAMA

Have students find a partner, and then have each student select three insults (two descriptive words and one noun) from the following list. These words will complete the sentence that starts: Thou art a
_____ _____ _____. (i.e. *Thou art a peevish, flea-bitten thorn*). When you sense they are ready, say, *Begin!*

+ *Descriptive words*: Peevish, wormy, beastly, filthy, uneducated, foul, saucy, yeasty, rank, worsted, wretched, grizzled, canker-blossom, dog-hearted, evil-eyed, lily-livered, wrinkled, green-eyed, evil-eyed, clay-brained, weathered, laughing-stock, fat-brained, worthless, flea-bitten, snail-paced, vile, rancid, decaying, green-sickness, etc.

+ *Noun*: snipe, witch, corpse, serpent, vulture, knave, rascal, monster, coward, beggar, dogfish, hedge-pig, newt, knotgrass, rogue, hag, savage, beast, brute, runyon, fenny snake, conniver, thorn, carrion, baggage, underling, mongrel, abomination, etc.

VOCAL/INSTRUMENTAL

Consider Drama Warm-Up #6, and with the class create a list of ugly sounds (horns honking, car alarms, an out-of-tune piano, the school fire alarm, fingernails on a chalkboard, etc.) Tell the class they will make a chorus of ugly sounds.

Teach the following drumming chant, and then divide the class into two groups: a drumming group and a vocal group. Everyone will have a turn to play the drums and vocalize their ugliest sounds. (May be used as a rhythm reading activity—not recorded.)

After each reading of the drum chant, cue in the improvisational Ugly Sounds Choir. Cut off when ready, and cue the drum chant in again. Repeat this call and response activity as many times as desired. Note that the drum chant and the choir never sing/play at the same time.

Macbeth Drumming With Ugly Sounds Choir

Louise Rogers

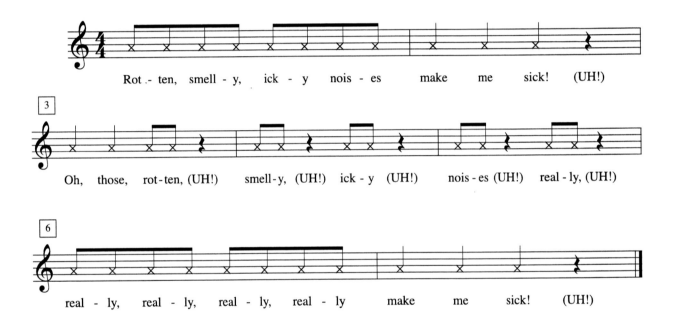

Rot - ten, smell - y, ick - y nois - es make me sick! (UH!)

Oh, those, rot-ten, (UH!) smell-y, (UH!) ick - y (UH!) nois - es (UH!) real - ly, (UH!)

real - ly, real - ly, real - ly, real - ly make me sick! (UH!)

WARM-UP #7

Explain that Shakespeare uses similes (comparisons that use *as* or *like*, such as, slow as molasses) and metaphors (comparisons without *as* or *like*, such as her eyes are sparkling jewels). See the list below for examples.

DRAMA

* Provide each student with a list of metaphors and similes. You can use the following list or additional lists generated by the classroom teacher and the class.

* Have each student select a partner.

- Have each pair select a metaphor or simile from the list, and decide how to pantomime the simile or metaphor. Allow time for them to plan, and then have each pair present their pantomime.

- After each pair performs, ask the class which metaphor or simile was dramatized. If it is not clear, challenge the students to add details.

Similes and Metaphors
- Busy as a bee
- Slow as molasses
- Quiet as a mouse
- Work like a beaver
- Stubborn as a mule
- Hard as a rock
- Sly as a fox
- Strong as an ox
- Graceful as a swan
- Hungry as a bear
- Sleeps like a log
- Shake like a leaf
- Mad as a wet hen
- Easy as pie
- Happy as a lark
- Flat like a pancake
- Quick as a wink
- Dead as a doornail
- He is such a pig
- He is a lion in battle
- Don't be a hog
- My love is a red, red rose
- All the world's a stage
- etc.

VOCAL/INSTRUMENTAL

Musical Similes and Metaphors

Refer to Drama Warm-Up #7 and engage the students in a conversation about metaphors and similes. Then, ask the students if they think there are similes and metaphors in music.

Discuss the following musical similes:
- *Musical as rain drops on a roof*
- *A Voice like a bird*
- *Sweet and musical as bright Apollo's lute strung with his hair*
  —William Shakespeare

Discuss the following musical metaphors:
- *The piano sings.*
- *The notes are alive.*
- *The walking bass.*

Ask the students if music can sound as *busy as a bee*, or as *brave as a bullfighter*, or as *sly as a fox*.

Can music be a red rose, a dream, or a shadow? Consider the following pieces (all available on iTunes) and ask the class if there is a simile or metaphor that fits: "Flight of the Bumblebee," "Moonlight Sonata," "March of the Toreadors," or "Pink Panther Theme."

Have the students create their own musical similes and/or metaphors in small groups, as a class, or individually. If done in small groups or individually, be sure to reconvene to share all of the ideas with the entire class. Remind the students to consider all of the different instruments. For example, drums, flute, trombone, gong, triangle, shaker, wood-stick, harp, kazoo, etc.

★ It's very helpful to have a list of musical terms available for the class to look at for this activity.

CORE ACTIVITIES

We suggest that prior to the start of the Core Activities, you work with the classroom teacher or librarian, and read Shakespeare's *Macbeth* retold by Bruce Coville, or "Macbeth" in *Shakespeare's Stories* by Beverly Birch, to familiarize the class with the story, characters, plots and themes. We also recommend Jennifer Mulherin's *Macbeth* for a simple scene-by-scene synopsis of the play.

We have included a bibliography at the end of this unit. We recommend for your reference the Cambridge School *Shakespeare's Macbeth* and Barron's *Simply Shakespeare*. In addition to the script, these two resources include suggested activities, explanations, vocabulary, and modern line-by-line interpretations.

Please note that in some cases we have simplified the dialogue, omitted lines from the original play, or shortened the scenes.

★ Students love to have a real cauldron and large pieces of black fabric to aid their characterizations!

ACTIVITY #1

Explain to the class that the first characters we meet in *Macbeth* are three witches, who are described as *withered and wild looking hags*. They're also referred to as the Weird Sisters, because they predict the future. (*Weird* or *wyrd* means *fate*; in Anglo-Saxon mythology, goddesses of destiny who predicted the future.)

DRAMA

Explain that their job as actors is to create unique personalities for the witches.

+ Instruct students to find a special place, close their eyes, and visualize a wide-open desolate place on a dark, stormy night with thunder, lightning, and sounds of evil everywhere. Have them visualize three witches entering into this atmosphere, and to imagine they are one of those witches. They are to decide what their witch looks like and how that witch moves and acts. Instruct them not to tell you, but just to visualize the character. Guide them with the following questions: "What do you look like? How do you move? Are you nervous? Do you have fourteen-inch fingernails? Are you the most powerful witch and want to impress the others with your power. Do you want to boss the others to make it clear that you're in charge? Do you hobble, strut, slink? Are you very young and flighty? Are you old and slow moving and trying to keep up with the others? Do you giggle constantly? Do you speak in dark whispers, or do you hiss, croak, mumble, babble, moan, groan, shriek, or screech? What are you wearing? What is your animal image (refer to Warm-Up #5, Exercise #2)? etc.

+ Have them open their eyes, and then slowly become the character they visualized. They are to "slip into the skins" of these evil characters by isolating parts of the body. Start with the forehead, eyes, nose, mouth, and chin. Then add the shoulders, elbows, wrists, and hands. Become the character in the waist, knees, ankles, and feet. Instruct them to become the character from the top of their heads to the tips of their toes. Have them freeze, stay in character, and walk through the stormy night. Guide them with questions such as: "Do you like the night and lightning, thunder, and the storm? Is it inspiring you to create a new potion or new spell? Is it enabling you to see into the future? *Freeze.*"

+ Instruct them to find a special space, and all speak together in a neutral voice, "When shall we three meet again? In thunder, lightning or in rain?" Then speak it in a dark whisper. Try it in different ways (hiss, croak, mumble, babble, moan, groan, shriek, etc.). Conclude with everyone speaking the lines as the unique personality they created for their character.

+ Distribute copies of the following first scene in *Macbeth*. Review unfamiliar vocabulary. Point out that in this scene we see the ability of the witches to predict the future. They indicate when the battle will be lost and won (before sunset).

+ If you would like to explain the scene before they read it, here is a summary: The Weird Sisters gather on a heath and question when they will meet again. They decide they will meet on the heath to greet Macbeth after the battle is over and one side has won and one side has lost. Their "familiars" (see vocabulary list) call them, and they leave chanting ominous words.

Vocabulary

- *Anon*: soon; later; at once; in a short time

- *Cauldron*: a large kettle

- *Ere*: before

- *Familiars*: spirits or demons in the disguise of animals that help the witches with their work

- *Foresee*: to see or know beforehand

- *Graymalkin* (gray cat) and *Paddock* (toad) are the first two witches' **familiars**; demons serving them in the form of a cat and a toad

- *Heath*: an open wasteland; a flat area of land with low shrubs

- *Hurly-burly*: commotion; noise of battle

- *Thane*: chief of a clan

THE SCENE FOR ACTIVITY #1

First Witch: When shall we three meet again,
In thunder, lightning, or in rain?

Second Witch: When the hurly-burly's done,
When the battle's lost and won.

Third Witch: That will be ere the set of sun.

First Witch: Where the place?

Second Witch: Upon the heath.

Third Witch: There to meet with Macbeth.

First Witch: I come, Graymalkin.

Second Witch: Paddock calls.

Third Witch: Anon!

All: Fair is foul, and foul is fair:
Hover through the fog and filthy air.

- After the class reads the scene together, divide the class into groups of three. Explain, that each group will plan how it wants to present this scene. Their job as actors and musicians is to establish the mood for this scene and foreshadow the evil and terror that follows. Each group is to:

> Decide who will play Witch #1, #2, #3, and then decide on unique personalities and characteristics for each witch.

> Plan and rehearse blocking. How will they enter into this desolate place? How do they leave? (cackling) Looking into the future, mumbling, or casting spells?

> Practice how they want to deliver the lines. Remind them of the Warm-Ups they did. They are to give meaning to the words they speak (inflection, emphasis, and how to make words such as *foul* and *hover* sound like their meaning).

- Allow time for each group to plan. As you check with each group, have each person describe in detail his or her witch's personality. When all groups are ready, have the class sit as an audience while each group presents its interpretation of the scene (scripts can be used, or they can improvise the dialogue).

- After all the groups have presented their interpretations of the scene, discuss with the class which group most effectively set the mood for evil. How did they do it? Was it with their voices? Their movement? Their characters? Their interpretation of the words? Which characterizations were the most believable? Why?

VOCAL

To accompany Drama Activity #1

Teach the two lower voices of "Spooky Forest Wind Song" (**CD Track 29**).

The wind blows and the forest is spooky. Talk with the class about sounds that you might hear in the dark, evil forest. Generate a list and practice, vocally, the sounds that the creatures or things make. For example: The Three Witches (remember their unique voices?), owls, birds of prey, a baboon, a wolf, a coyote, footsteps, animals running, a scream, thunder and lightning, etc.
Before the witches enter (see Drama Activity #1), set the eerie scene with the "Spooky Forest Wind Song" and the improvised sounds of the night.
Note: As the witches enter and recite their lines, the wind vocals and sound effects can continue but very softly in the background.

Spooky Forest Wind Song

Louise Rogers

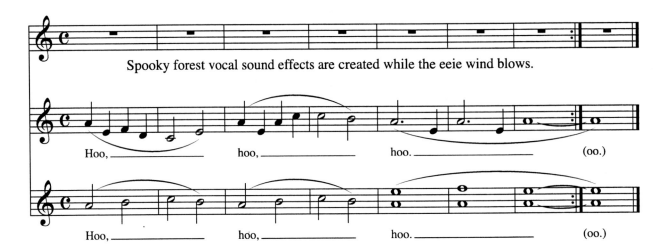

Spooky forest vocal sound effects are created while the eeie wind blows.

Hoo,   hoo,   hoo.   (oo.)

Hoo,   hoo,   hoo.   (oo.)

Repeat as many times as desired.
The bottom two voices sing on the sound of the eerie wind.
The top line is reserved for the spooky sounds of the forest.
Refer to the list generated by the class. Sound effects can
be sung as solos or the class can be divided into groups.
The last time the song is sung should be culmination of
all of the sounds of the forest with the wind blowing eerily
in the background.

ACTIVITY #2

> ★ There is a condensed compilation of the first scene and this scene in Lorraine Cohen's "Scenes for Young Actors," if you prefer to use a simpler condensed version.

Explain to the class that in order to continue to develop the characters of the witches, we're going to fast-forward to part of a scene that happens in Act 4, Scene 1.

In this scene, the witches meet again in a desolate place (a cavern) to weave their spells. They chant and dance around a fiery cauldron, with thunder and lightning in the background.

DRAMA

Distribute copies of the following scene, and review unfamiliar vocabulary.

Have the class read together the scene aloud, and then divide the class into groups of four (three witches and Hecate). Allow them time to plan how they want to present this scene.

Some suggestions to guide them through their planning stage:

+ Since Macbeth takes these characters seriously, have them focus on creating believable characters, and giving believability to the words they speak.

+ Remind them of the Warm-Ups and how they gave meaning to words. How can they make the word *cool* sound as if it is cooling a fiery brew? When they chant, "Double, double, toil and trouble, fire burn and cauldron bubble," challenge them to decide what they want those words to accomplish. Do they speak the words to conjure up evil, or to coax the pot to boil faster, or make the fire higher?

+ Focus them on believable and detailed pantomime. How do they hold the toe of a frog, or the wool of a bat, etc.? Where do they get the ingredients?

+ Challenge them to experiment with different ways to move and speak.

Vocabulary

- *Adder's fork:* poisonous snake

- *Blind-worm:* slow worm; small harmless lizard

- *Brinded:* streaked with color, or striped

- *Charm:* spell

- *Entrails:* guts

- *Fenny snake:* slimy snake found in a fen (low, flat, swampy land)

- *Harpier:* name of a familiar (see vocabulary in Activity #1); a harpy had a woman's face and a bird's body; a demon

- *Hath:* has

- *Hecate:* goddess of witchcraft

- *Hedge-pig:* hedgehog

- *Howlet:* young owl

- *Locks:* doors

- *Mewed:* meowed

- *Prickings of my thumb:* tingling in my thumbs

- *'Tis time:* it's time

- *Thrice:* three

- *Wound up:* done; ready for action

THE SCENE FOR ACTIVITY #2

First Witch: Thrice the brinded cat hath mewed.

Second Witch: Thrice and once the hedge-pig whined.

Third Witch: Harpier cries, 'tis time, 'tis time.

First Witch: Round about the cauldron go.
In the poisoned entrails throw.

All: Double, double, toil and trouble,
Fire burn and cauldron bubble.

Second Witch: Fillet of a fenny snake,
In the cauldron boil and bake.
Eye of newt and toe of frog,
Wool of bat and tongue of dog,
Adder's fork and blind-worm's sting,
Lizard's leg and howlet's wing,
For a charm of powerful trouble,
Like a hell broth boil and bubble.

All: Double, double, toil and trouble,
Fire burn and cauldron bubble.

Second Witch: Cool it with a baboon's blood,
Then the charm is firm and good.

(Enter Hecate, and three other witches)
(**Note:** Students can imagine the three other witches)

Hecate: O well done! I commend your pains,
And every one shall share in the gains;
And now about the cauldron sing
Like elves and fairies in a ring,
Enchanting all that you put in.

(Music, and a song)

(Exit Hecate and the other three witches)

Second Witch: By the pricking of my thumbs,
Something wicked this way comes.
Open locks, whoever knocks.

VOCAL/INSTRUMENTAL ⊙ Track 30

"Black Spirits": To Accompany Drama Activity #2

- Set-up all xylophones with G, B♭, D, F♯, G (high). Glockenspiels should replace F natural with F♯.

- Orff instrument parts should be taught by rote. Remove all of the bars except the ones they will be playing. Teach the xylophone parts first and add snaps for glockenspiel parts. Add log drum improvisation.

- To create the cauldron music use xylophones only so that a shortened sound occurs. Metallophones ring too long. The log drum is used to improvise bubble sounds as the witches work on their potion. Students might have additional ideas for bubble sounds.

- Use the voice to help create the sounds of the bubbling cauldron as the instruments are playing. Will this be a loud sound? Will it be a low or a high sound? Will you sing it differently if you are the only bubble or if the entire class is bubbles? Can a bubbling pot sound evil and sinister vs. happy and peppy?

- Students should decide if the music is the right dynamic level for the scene and come up with an appropriate tempo. Ask xylophones and glockenspiels to experiment with playing on the handles of their mallets to see if they like the sound quality better for spooky cauldron music.

Black Spirits

Kimberly McCord

ACTIVITY #3

Explain that now that they have met the three witches, we're going back to the beginning of the play. Summarize this scene:

While the witches await Macbeth, they discuss the evil spells they have put on people, and the revenge the first witch will get on a sailor's wife who ignored her. When they hear a drum that indicates Macbeth has arrived, they join hands and dance, (or some movement pattern of three sets of movement to add up to nine) to make the spell ready for action.

Macbeth, who is Thane of Glamis and a great warrior, is returning with his friend Banquo from battle. They have succeeded in defeating the enemy. They come across the witches and wonder who or what they are. The witches predict that Macbeth will be Thane of Cawdor and then King. Banquo then asks them to speak to him. They predict that Banquo's sons will be kings, but not Banquo.

DRAMA

Distribute the following scene and review unfamiliar vocabulary. Have the class read the following scene aloud.

Vocabulary

- *Aroint thee:* be off with you; begone

- *Aught:* anything

- *Charmed:* to use magic spells, to cast a spell on

- *Choppy:* chapped, or gruesome

- *Fantastical:* imaginary; illusion

- *Favours:* favors

- *Forres:* a castle in Scotland where Duncan lives

- *Glamis:* (pronounced Glahms), small village in Eastern Scotland

- *Hemlock:* poisonous plant

- *Insane root:* plant thought to cause insanity

- *Posters:* speedy travelers

- *Rump-fed:* fat one

- *Runyon:* hag

- *Sieve:* kitchen strainer

- *The Tiger:* a merchant ship

- *Thither:* there

- *Wound up:* done; ready for action

Distribute the following scene, and review unfamiliar vocabulary. Have the class read the following scene aloud.

THE SCENE FOR ACTIVITY #3

(A heath. Thunder. Enter the three witches.)

First Witch: Where hast thou been, sister?

Second Witch: Killing swine.

Third Witch: Sister, where thou?

First Witch: A sailor's wife had chestnuts in her lap
And munched, and munched, and munched.

'Give me', said I.
'Aroint thee, witch', the rump-fed ronyon cries.
Her husband's off to sea as captain of the *Tiger*:
But in a sieve I'll thither sail,
And like a rat without a tail,
I'll do, I'll do, and I'll do. (*Means: I'll make trouble and get revenge*)

(*Drum beats*)

Third Witch: A drum, a drum!
Macbeth doth come.

All Witches: (*chant*) The Weird Sisters, hand in hand,
Posters of the sea and land,
Thus do go about, about,
Thrice to thine, and thrice to mine,
And thrice again, to make up nine.
Peace! The charm's wound up.

(*Enter Macbeth and Banquo*)

Macbeth: So foul and fair a day I have not seen.

Banquo (*sees the witches and questions whether they're real or not; whether they live on Earth; and whether you can speak to them*):
How far is it called to Forres? (*sees the witches*) What are these,
So withered, and so wild in their attire,
That look not like inhabitants of the Earth,
And yet are on it? Are you alive? Or are you aught
That man may question? You seem to understand me,
By each at once her choppy finger laying
Upon her skinny lips; you should be women,
And yet your beards forbid me to interpret
That you are so.

Macbeth: Speak, if you can: What are you?

First Witch: All hail, Macbeth! Hail to thee, Thane of Glamis!

Second Witch: All hail Macbeth! Hail to thee, Thane of Cawdor!

Third Witch: All hail Macbeth! That shalt be king hereafter.

Banquo: If you can look into the seeds of time,
And say which grain will grow and which will not,
Speak to me, who neither beg nor fear
Your favours nor your hate.

First Witch: Hail!

Second Witch: Hail!

Third Witch: Hail!

(*The witches look at Banquo*)

First Witch: Lesser than Macbeth, and greater.

Second Witch: Not so happy, yet much happier.

Third Witch: Thou shalt get kings, though thou be none:
So all hail Macbeth and Banquo!

First Witch: Banquo and Macbeth, all hail!

Macbeth: Tell me more!
I know I am Thane of Glamis,
But how can I be Thane of Cawdor? He is alive.
And how will I be king?

(*The witches vanish*)

After the reading of the scene:

You can have the class read the scene together and then do the following improvisation to conclude the scene; or divide the class into groups and have them plan, rehearse, and perform the scene as they did in Activity #2, and then conclude with the following improvisation.

Improvisation

After the witches vanish, have volunteers improvise the conversation between Macbeth and Banquo. What are their reactions? Do they believe they saw witches, or do they think they're imagining it, or that they themselves are going crazy or exhausted from battle? Do they think the witches are lying, testing them, or telling the truth that Macbeth will be king? After all, King Duncan is alive, and his son Malcolm is the rightful heir if anything happens to King Duncan. Does Banquo try to convince Macbeth to ignore the witches' prophecies, but Macbeth thinks there might be truth in their words? Do they believe in fate or free will? What does Banquo think about what they said about *his* future?

Group Work

If the class works in groups, challenge them to carefully plan how they will speak and move as they go around the cauldron. Remind them that they have put all the ingredients in the pot, completed their "double double" chant, and now with their bodies, actions, dance and movements, they must make the potion work. "Peace, the charm's wound up," indicates to stop, because the potion is ready.

Challenge them to use their bodies to help make the evil spell "wound up." Remind the groups that when they predict the future, they need to be haunting and believable in order to set Macbeth's mind thinking about a future as King, and to stir murderous thoughts.

INSTRUMENTAL (Track 28)

"How Weird Are These Sisters?"

Explain to the class that after they learn the instrumental piece "How Weird Are These Sisters?" (**CD Track 28**) they will add the witches' voices. The piece will then accompany Drama Activity #3 above.

Identify where the peak of the scene is and how to best illustrate that with music. What instruments might they use? How fast or slow should the music go? How loud or soft should the music be?

Practice without the musicians first and then add the actors. Discuss each time how well the music enhances or detracts from the scene. What can be done to improve it? Try it again until the students are satisfied. If students are having trouble playing the music and noticing the actors, you might video it and play it back so they can see and hear better, and then make edits.

Teach the piece, "How Weird Are These Sisters?"

+ Soprano xylophone and metallophones should remove C's and G's.

+ Teach the bass xylophone part through body percussion by patting right, left, right, right (to the outside of right thigh), right (front of thigh). Left pat stays on the front of thigh. Select a student(s) who has mastered the body percussion part and transfer to bass xylophone. Have players play the part.

+ First divide the class into two groups. Pat with the left hand on count 1, and the right hand on count 3 while counting out loud. Have the students on your left play with you on count 1 and the students on your right pat on count 3. Transfer to bass and alto metallophones. Basses play on count 1 and alto on count 3. Add with bass xylophone part.

+ Next teach the short chant "hov-er through the fog, si-lence." Have students pat the rhythm on their thighs as they say the chant. Have them drop the word *silence* and think it in their heads. They should also be silent and not pat on that word. Transfer to alto xylophone.

+ Play all parts together layering them in BX, BM, AM, AX.

Now we need to develop our soundtrack further. Ask students to think about other unpitched percussion that might complement the soundtrack. The students should decide which instruments they would like to use and where they will play.

Some decisions need to be made about where the music will occur and for how long. If it is as background music for the scene, the musicians will need to decide how many players will play and if the piece repeats.

> ★ The students may decide to use this piece again later in the play.

Students might elect to add improvisation on the soprano instruments. Should just one or several persons improvise? Do they like the sound of the xylophone or metallophone? They might also decide to compose a melody that is played by the soprano instruments. All of these parts need to be notated on the score.

Select a conductor if there is a student interested in trying to conduct the piece. Consider making the finished score an overhead so everyone can see it.

VOCAL Track 28

Review the witches' voices that the class created in Vocal Warm-Up #1. Now, put these voices together with the instrumental music, "How Weird Are These Sisters?" (**CD Track 28**). Explain to the class that the witches' cackling will begin over the instrumental accompaniment at the beginning of the scene before the witches begin talking. Some members of the class will play the instruments. Ask for volunteers to be the witches. Witches should laugh one at a time and then together as per instructions below, cackling in their individual voices.

+ Each witch has two measures by themselves.

+ Then they "trade" measures in an engaging and expressively evil conversation of witch cackles.

+ The piece ends with all three witches cackling and laughing together in their distinctively different voices.

+ Piece/scene ends with a cue from Witch #1 and one final laugh from all three witches.

> ★ The three cackling witches for the soundtrack and the three witches in the dramatic scene may be played by different students. Each witch may even be sung/played by small groups.

ACTIVITY #4

Explain to the class that they will create original soliloquies, and improvise dialogue for the next few scenes. Instruct them to listen to the description of the scenes so they can decide which scene they'd like to improvise, or which soliloquy they'd like to deliver.

DRAMA

Students can work in groups and improvise each of the following scenes, and include asides and soliloquies, or you can focus on individual student's improvised soliloquies for each scene. We have included suggestions for the soliloquies.

THE SCENES FOR ACTIVITY #4

Scene 1

After Macbeth and Banquo leave the witches, they continue their journey. A messenger sent by King Duncan appears out of the fog and hails Macbeth, "Hail, Thane of Cawdor!" He explains that the Thane of Cawdor betrayed King Duncan and is condemned to die. King Duncan is rewarding Macbeth for his great action in battle, and making Macbeth the Thane of Cawdor.

Macbeth and Banquo realize that the witches' first prophecy has come true. Banquo says in an aside, "What! Can the devil speak true?" (Did the witches really speak the truth?) Macbeth thinks there may be truth in the prediction that he will be king.

The scene ends with Banquo advising Macbeth, "Be not too eager. Remember, the power of darkness may use a bit of truth to lure men to doom."

Soliloquy idea: Imagine Macbeth is alone. Improvise his soliloquy. What are his thoughts? The Weird Sisters prophesized that he would become Thane of Cawdor, and that is now a reality. Does this mean he is destined to become king? The thought appeals to him, and for a moment he thinks about a plan to get rid of King Duncan. However, Macbeth knows right from wrong and dismisses the thought.

Scene 2

The men set up camp. Macbeth writes to his wife, Lady Macbeth, and tells her what has happened. Throughout the night, he struggles with his thoughts. He thinks again of what the witches predicted. As he thinks about becoming king, murderous thoughts enter his mind. He is torn between his sense of morality and his ambition.

Soliloquy idea: Improvise soliloquies that capture Macbeth's thoughts. Focus on his moral dilemma. Consider whether it is the witches' predictions that turn his thoughts towards becoming king at all costs, or his own ambitions. Is fate determining what he will do, or is he master of his own destiny?

Scene 3

Lady Macbeth receives the letter from Macbeth, and her mind starts thinking about the witches' predictions. She is afraid that Macbeth is too kind and soft-hearted, and will not take matters into his own hands. She says, "I fear your nature, my husband, is too full of the milk of human kindness." She knows he is ambitious and wants to be king, but he will want to win it rightfully and morally, and will not commit acts of murder. She resolves that she will have to encourage him to action ("I shall have to urge thee on to do what must be done").

Soliloquy idea: Instruct students who volunteer for this scene to read what they think the letter says, and then deliver a soliloquy that captures Lady Macbeth's thoughts.

Note to Teachers: Once students select which scenes or soliloquies they want to work on, you can start the improvisations immediately, or allow time for planning.

VOCAL/INSTRUMENTAL

For ideas on musical soliloquies, see Vocal/Instrumental Warm-Up #3.

ACTIVITY #5

Let's Improvise Together!

Note: This activity provides an opportunity for everyone to improvise together! It combines drama, vocal, and instrumental improvisation, and provides an opportunity to include the classroom teacher. It can be a true collaborative effort. The classroom teacher can guide students in their use of language, metaphors, similes, and how to structure the scene with a beginning, middle and conclusion. It is also an opportunity for students to share their work with other classes.

Procedure:

If you would like to continue to cover the entire play, you can either work scene by scene with the entire class, or divide the class into groups of approximately six to eight students, and have each group work on a different scene. Some students can be the actors, and others can be the musicians.

If you decide to have the class work in groups, provide the class with the plot outline that we have provided at the end of this unit. Each group will select a different scene, and decide how they want to present the scene to the class. They can improvise dialogue or use some of the actual dialogue from the play (see recommended adaptations in the bibliography at the end of the unit). They must figure out a way to incorporate drama *and* music.

Each group should include in their presentation:
- at least five Shakespearean words or phrases (There is a suggested list at the end of the unit.)
- at least one metaphor or simile
- at least one line or phrase from the actual play
- at least one aside or soliloquy
- musical improvisations (*see the following Vocal/Instrumental Instructions*)

★ After each group presents its scene, the class can evaluate the scene for: effectiveness of characterization, use of voices, movement, and how music enhanced the scene, etc.

VOCAL/INSTRUMENTAL Track 28 Track 29 Track 30

For the remaining scenes of *Macbeth*, the students will create their own soundtrack: melodies or sound effects to accompany the scenes. Consider the musical elements that have helped to shape the story so far.

- In the first activity, the "Spooky Forest Wind Song" (**CD Track 29**) provided an eerie mysterious and spooky soundtrack. The students improvised drumming and vocal sounds to create a dark and evil forest.

- In the second activity, the students learned the instrumental song "Black Spirits" (**CD Track 30**). They improvised on the log drum and with the voice to help create the bubbling sounds of the evil brew in the cauldron.

- In the third activity, the students learned the instrumental piece, "How Weird Are These Sisters?" (**CD Track 28**). Individual and unique witch voices were created by the students for each of the three witches. The witches cackled as the instruments played. They conversed with each other by exchanging improvised cackles every other measure.

Musical Elements to consider:
- Dynamics (loud/soft)
- Vocal improvisation (a vocal melody or sound effect that is spontaneous and new)
- Instrumental improvisation (an instrumental melody or sound effect that is spontaneous and new)
- Repetitive musical motif (ostinato) that provides a stable foundation for improvisations
- Crescendos, decrescendos (getting louder and softer)
- Staccato, legato (short and jumpy sounds vs. long and smooth sounds)
- Tempo (how fast or slow was the piece?)
- Instrumentation (what instruments were used)
- Vocal arrangement (how many voices are singing?)
- Lyrics/no lyrics (does the piece have words?)
- Beginning and ending of piece
- Ask the students for more ideas

The musicians should work carefully with the actors, being mindful of the following questions:

- Where is the action?
- Where is the climax?
- What is the mood – sad, happy, scary, evil, sinister, mysterious, funny?
- Does the entire scene need music? Would some sections be better without music?

How to start:

- Encourage students to create the stable foundation, the ostinato that captures the essence of the scene.

- Instruct the students to notate their ostinato so they will remember it. If they cannot write it using standard music notation, they will need to create an alternative way to remember what they wrote. Remind the students that the ostinato is always a repeated pattern, and notating the pattern will be important and helpful.

- Add improvisation – vocal and/or instrumental.

- As the scene develops, add from musical elements listed above.

- New ostinatos may be created for each scene.

★ Students may use one of the ostinatos created in "Spooky Forest Wind Song," "Black Spirit," or "How Weird Are These Sisters?".

Creative Extensions

- Put Lady Macbeth or Macbeth on trial. Can she plead insanity? Can Macbeth blame the witches?

- Put the witches on trial. Can they be blamed for starting Macbeth on his path to evil?

- Create original chants (instead of "double, double, toil and trouble, etc.") for the witches.

- The class can work in groups on newscasts that bring the listeners/viewers up to date on latest events in Macbeth.

- Interview the main characters for a talk show. Have the class develop interview questions such as, "Did you really think you could get away with it?" "Why did you listen to the witches?" etc.

- Refer to the bibliography. Books such as Shakespeare, Yes You Can, include follow-up activities.

Shakespeare's Language to be Used in Activity #5

(or in any improvisation throughout the unit)

- **Abomination**: thing producing great dislike or disgust
- **Alas**: too bad
- **Art**: are
- **Bestride**: sit or ride astride (with a leg on each side); to mount
- **Betimes**: early
- **Bid**: ask
- **Canst**: cannot
- **Cast**: make
- **Come hither**: come here
- **Dearest**: dear
- **Didst**: did
- **Doth**: does
- **Drops of sorrow**: tears
- **Durst**: dare
- **Entreat**: beg
- **Enow**: enough
- **Ere**: before
- **Exeunt**: exit, leave
- **Fain**: gladly
- **Fantastical**: imaginary
- **Feat**: notable act or deed; act of courage
- **Foresee**: to see beforehand
- **For want of**: for lack of
- **Fraught**: full-of; filled with
- **Harbinger**: announcer

- **Hast**: has
- **Hence**: thus, so
- **Hie**: hurry
- **Hither**: here; to or toward this place
- **Ho**: hello
- **Hurly-burly**: noise of battle; commotion
- **I beseech you**: please
- **I know not**: I do not know
- **I prithee**: I beg
- **Impart**: tell
- **Methinks**: I think
- **Naught**: worthless
- **Nay**: no
- **O'er**: over
- **Presently**: at once
- **I Prithee**: I pray you; I beg you
- **Seest**: see
- **Spent**: exhausted
- **Stay**: wait
- **Swelt'red**: sweated
- **Thee**: plural for you
- **Thine**: possessive for your (thine kingdom)
- **Thither**: there; in that direction; to or toward a place
- **Thou**: singular pronoun for you (how art thou?)

- **Thou'rt**: thou art (you are)
- **Thrice**: three
- **Thus**: so
- **'Tis**: it is
- **Thy**: your (possessive)
- **Unfold**: reveal
- **What means you?** What do you mean?
- **Wherefore**: why; "Wherefore art thou Romeo?" (Why is your name Romeo?)
- **Wherein**: in what place?
- **Whet**: warn
- **Whilst**: while

Note: Many words end in "th" or "st" (shouldt, canst, didst) (if thou speak'st false)

THE SCENES FOR ACTIVITY #5

Plot Outline to Distribute to Each Group

Act 1, Scene 5

Macbeth tells Lady Macbeth that King Duncan will be visiting that night and leaving in the morn. Lady, Macbeth replies, "Never shall that morning come, my lord." (*O never shall sun that morrow see!*) She instructs Macbeth to look natural and innocent in order to deceive everyone. (*Your face, my lord is like a book wherein men may read strange matters. Bear welcome in your eye, your hand, your tongue; look like the innocent flower, but be the serpent under't.*)

Macbeth suggests that they speak further about this, but she tells him to just look innocent, welcome everyone, and leave the rest to her.

Act 1, Scene 6

The castle is filled with excitement over King Duncan's visit. King Duncan arrives with his sons Malcolm and Donalbain, as well as Banquo, Macduff, Ross and other attendants. Duncan comments on the pleasant surroundings and sweet air. Lady Macbeth, who acts like a gracious hostess, greets him. He asks her to lead him to Macbeth, whom he loves highly, and whom he shall continue to honor.

Act 1, Scene 7

Macbeth is alone and tries to talk himself out of the murder of King Duncan (*I should bar the door against his murderer, not bear the knife myself.*) He knows that as his host he should protect King Duncan, and prevent his murder. He is also scared about the consequences. Duncan is his cousin, and is an honest and good king. Also, does he really have any reason to kill Duncan other than his own ambitions because of the witches' prophecy? As he contemplates the murder he says, "If it were done, when 'tis done, then 'twere well it were done quickly...."

He tells Lady Macbeth, "We will proceed no further in this business." However, Lady Macbeth makes him think he is a coward and convinces him to take action. (*Screw your courage to the sticking place* (to its height) *and we'll not fail!*)

She reveals her plot to Macbeth. She'll give wine to the King's guards so they'll fall asleep, and then Macbeth will kill the unguarded Duncan. Macbeth is appalled, but afraid to admit to Lady Macbeth that he is a coward, so he agrees. He suggests that they use the guards' daggers for the crime, to make the guards look guilty.

Act 2, Scene 1

Banquo, in a room of his own at the castle, has been thinking of the witches' predictions. He senses that something terrible is going to happen.

Macbeth lays awake waiting for the time to come to kill Duncan. He has a vision of a dagger which he tries to clasp, but can't grasp. He keeps telling himself he is imagining things because he is afraid. He keeps seeing the dagger. The second time he sees it with blood on it.

Note: Since this is a famous soliloquy, the group might want to use part of it in its improvisation of the scene.

"Is this a dagger which I see before me,

The handle toward my hand? Come, let me clutch thee! (*He reaches, but there is nothing there*)

I have thee not, and yet I see thee still.

Art thou not, fatal vision, sensible

To feeling as to sight? Or art thou but

A dagger of the mind, a false creation,

Proceeding from the heat-oppressed brain?"

He hears a bell, which is Lady Macbeth's signal to kill Duncan (*I go, and it is done.*)

Act 2, Scene 2

Lady Macbeth has seen to it that the guards are drunk and asleep, and has placed their daggers near them for Macbeth to use for the murder. She comments that if King Duncan did not resemble her father as he slept, she'd have murdered him herself. She waits while Macbeth enters Duncan's chambers.

Macbeth staggers out of the chamber holding blood stained daggers. Lady Macbeth questions why he didn't smear the guards with the blood and leave the daggers near them to make them look like the murderers.

Macbeth is horrified with what he has done. His conscience bothers him, and he imagines he hears a voice saying he has murdered sleep and will sleep no more (*I thought I heard a voice cry 'Sleep no more! Macbeth doth murder sleep'*). Macbeth says he cannot go back and look at what he has done.

Lady Macbeth says, "Infirm (weak) of purpose! Give me the daggers," and she hurries off to complete the task. When she returns, she tells him they need to get washed and look as if they were sleeping.

Suddenly, there is a loud knocking at the gates. The scene ends with Macbeth saying, "Wake Duncan with thy knocking! I would thou couldst!"

Act 2, Scenes 3 and 4

The castle porter is in a drunken sleep, and has been slow to open the gates. In fact, "Knock, knock, knock! Who's there?" is repeated several times throughout the scene, as the porter imagines himself the keeper of the gates of Hell, welcoming all kinds of people such as con artists who lied under oath. He tries to determine who is knocking. The knocking gets louder and louder.

The porter finally opens the door, and Macbeth, cleaned and dressed, greets Macduff and Lennox, two noblemen. Macduff tells Macbeth that Duncan requested he be there early to awake him. Macbeth shows him to King Duncan's chamber, and leaves Macduff to go in himself. Macduff enters to wake the king. He returns horror stricken screaming, "Horror, horror, horror! Awake, awake! Ring the alarum bell! Murder and treason!"

Duncan's sons Malcolm and Donalbain arrive at the scene. Lennox tells them the guards are suspects, as their hands, faces and daggers are smeared with blood. Macbeth enters and states that he just killed the two guards because they killed Duncan.

Macduff eyes Macbeth with suspicion. Lady Macbeth enters and asks what's happening. Macduff replies, "Oh gentle lady, it's not right for you to hear the words," and tells her.

Macbeth becomes King of Scotland, because Malcolm and Donalbain, King Duncan's sons, flee in fear they are also in danger. However, because they flee, they are suspected of the murder of their father. People wonder if the two sons urged the guards to kill their father so they could rule.

Macduff is uneasy about Macbeth's sudden accession to the throne, and does not go to the coronation. He returns to his home in Fife.

Act 3, Scenes 1, 2, 3

Banquo, alone, thinks about Macbeth's sudden ascension to the throne, and wonders if Macbeth has done evil to accomplish it. He suspects he killed Duncan.

Macbeth thinks about his fear of Banquo. Banquo is bold and wise. Macbeth also fears the truth of the witch's prophecy that Banquo's heirs will be kings.

Macbeth decides to hold a banquet at his castle, asks Banquo to be his guest of honor, and then arranges for Banquo's murder. He convinces the murderers that they're not well off in life because of Banquo, and if they get rid of Banquo, they will have Macbeth's lasting friendship.

Macbeth asks Lady Macbeth (he has not shared his plans with her) to be extra pleasant to Banquo that night. Macbeth seems upset. Lady Macbeth thinks it's because of the murder of Duncan, and says, "What's done, is done."

Act 3, Scene 4

When the banquet begins, Macbeth is informed by one of the murderers that Banquo has been murdered, but Banquo's son Fleance escaped. Macbeth resumes the festivities and as he raises his glass to toast, he sees the bloody ghost of Banquo sitting in his seat. He is frightened and disturbed.

The ghost vanishes, and when it appears again, it stands behind Macbeth. No one else sees it and wonders about Macbeth's strange behavior as he says, "Quit my sight. Hence horrible shadow…Go. Get back to the grave…."

Lady Macbeth makes excuses for Macbeth's behavior, and tells the guests he is not well. She explains that this is a condition he has always had. She dismisses the guests.

When the guests leave, Macbeth insists on seeing the witches again.

Note: *The ghost does not speak in the play, but students can create dialogue if desired.*

Act 3, Scene 5

Hecate, the boss and source of the three witches' powers, is angry with them because they gave Macbeth prophecies without confiding in her. She feels they're wasting their time on him because he is selfish. She orders them to meet her in the morning where Macbeth will learn his destiny. She will work a spell that will cause magical spirits to trick Macbeth with illusions.

Act 3, Scene 6

Lennox and another Scottish lord discuss the latest happenings. Lennox thinks Fleance (Banquo's son), must be the murderer because he fled the scene. The lord reports that Macduff has gone to England, where Malcolm is staying, to try to raise an army to unseat Macbeth and free Scotland from Macbeth's bloody rule.

Act 4, Scene 1

Macbeth finds the witches in a cave concocting a brew (this is the scene we did in the beginning with "Fillet of a fenny snake…"). He tells them he wants to know the truth of the future.

They raise three apparitions:

1) An Armed Head (head with an armored helmet) that warns Macbeth to beware Macduff, Thane of Fife;

2) A Bloody Child, which warns that no one of woman born will harm Macbeth; and

3) A Child Crowned, bearing a tree in his hand, who says that Macbeth will not be defeated until Birnam Wood comes to Dunsinane (the location of Macbeth's castle).

Macbeth inquires if Banquo's descendants will be kings, and they show Macbeth an apparition of a line of kings all resembling Banquo.

At the end of the scene Macbeth learns that Macduff has fled to England to join Malcolm, one of Duncan's sons, to organize an army against Macbeth. Macbeth decides to kill Macduff's family to get revenge.

Act 4, Scene 2

Lady Macduff is upset because her husband left her and her son. Ross tries to convince her that her husband knew what he was doing and times are dangerous and cruel now under Macbeth's tyranny. He believes things will change and get better. At the end of the scene Lady Macduff and her son are murdered.

Act 4, Scene 3

Macduff seeks out Malcolm and urges him to depose Macbeth and take over Scotland's rule. Malcolm at first distrusts Macduff. He thinks he might be a spy for Macbeth and has been sent by Macbeth to kill him. After all, Macduff was a friend of Macbeth, and Macbeth used to be an honest man. Eventually, he is convinced, and orders an army to get ready.

Ross reports that revolts have already begun under Macbeth's rule.

Macduff learns his family has been murdered, and is determined to kill Macbeth himself.

Act 5, Scene 1

Lady Macbeth behaves oddly. Her attendant (or gentlewoman) fetches the doctor to see what illness could make the Queen leave her bed, wander the halls, and keep a candle by her side. She explains that ever since Macbeth went to war, Lady Macbeth gets out of bed, puts on her nightgown, unlocks her closet, takes out a paper, folds it, writes, reads it and seals it and goes back to sleep. Yet she does this all fast asleep. When the doctor asks what Lady Macbeth says, the gentlewoman will not tell him.

The attendant and the doctor watch as Lady Macbeth walks with a candle in her hand as if in a trance. As she sleepwalks, she talks to herself about Duncan's murder, and constantly rubs her hands to try to wash the blood from her hands. Her guilt has driven her mad. "Out, damned spot! Out I say. Yet who would have thought the old gentleman to have had so much blood in him?" She continues while the doctor observes her, "The Thane of Fife had a wife: where is she now?.....What, will these hands ne'er be clean? Here's the smell of the blood still. And all the perfumes of Arabia will not sweeten this little hand. O, O, O!"

The doctor explains that this disease is beyond his practice. He thinks she needs a priest rather than a doctor.

Act 5, Scenes 2, 3

Macbeth learns that the English army is near and asks for his armor, and orders more cavalry sent out. The doctor tells Macbeth that Lady Macbeth is troubled with visions that keep her from sleeping. Macbeth tells him to find some drug to ease her troubling thoughts.

Act 5, Scene 4

Macbeth sets up defenses around Dunsinane castle. Most of his noblemen and soldiers have joined the other side against him. He is certain he will win because of the witches prediction that he will not be defeated until Birnam Wood comes to Dunsinane, and he knows that a forest cannot move.

However, the soldiers have all met at Birnam Wood, where each one has been given a branch of a tree to hide the size of the army as they move forward to attack.

Act 5, Scene 5

As Macbeth is preparing for battle, he learns that Lady Macbeth has killed herself. Alone, he reflects on how meaningless life is.

Note: *Since this is a famous soliloquy, the group who selects to improvise this scene, should include part of Macbeth's speech:*

"Tomorrow, and tomorrow, and tomorrow; creeps in this petty pace from day to day, to the last syllable of recorded time: and all our yesterdays have lighted fools the way to dusty death. Out, out brief candle! Life's but a walking shadow, a poor player that struts and frets his hour upon this stage, and then is heard no more. It is a tale told by an idiot, full of sound and fury, signifying nothing."

A messenger bursts in on him while he is reflecting on the meaninglessness of life, to tell him that as he stood watch upon the hill, he looked towards Birnam and he thought the Wood began to move. Macbeth then learns that Birnam Wood appears to move. "To Arms! To Arms! Ring the alarms," Macbeth orders.

Act 5, Scenes 6, 7, 8

Malcolm and Macduff begin their attack. Macbeth's castle is taken. He meets Macduff on the battlefield. The two fight fiercely with swords, but Macbeth tells him he wastes his energy because he will not be defeated by one of woman born. Macduff informs him that he was not born as normal men, but taken early from his mother's womb by a surgeon (Caesarian, so he was "not of woman born").

Macduff kills Macbeth and brings his head to Malcolm.

Peace is restored to Scotland, and Malcolm, the rightful heir, is crowned king.

RESOURCES for SHAKESPEARE UNIT

Aliki. *William Shakespeare and the Globe*. Harper Collins Publishers, 1999. An easy to read introduction to Shakespeare's life, the Globe Theatre, Elizabethan England.

Birch, Beverly. *Shakespeare's Stories. The Tragedies*. New York, New York: Peter Bedrick Books, 1988. Descriptive retelling of the Shakespeare's plays in story form.

Burdette, Lois. *Macbeth For Kids*. Ontario, Canada: Black Moss Press, 1995. **Note:** This author has also written a series, *Shakespeare Can Be Fun* geared for the younger elementary grades (grades 2 and 3) that includes other plays, as well as a book about Shakespeare's life and times.

Cambridge School. *Shakespeare. Macbeth*. Edited by Rex Gibson. New York: Cambridge University Press, 1998. The text is on one page, and writing, acting, and creative activities are on the other page. At the end of the text, there is a section that includes information on Shakespeare, his language, themes, the Globe theatre, etc.

Cohen, Lorraine. *Scenes for Young Actors*. New York, New York: Aron Books, Imprint of Harper Collins, 1973. Includes a scene with the three witches.

Coville, Bruce. *William Shakespeare's Macbeth*. New York, New York: Dial Books, 1997. This is our favorite story adaptation (with illustrations) of the play. He has also adapted *Midsummer Night's Dream* and *The Tempest*.

Egan, Lorraine Hopping. *Teaching Shakespeare. Yes You Can*. New York, New York: Scholastic Professional Books, 1998. Simple activities to teach any of Shakespeare's plays. Includes suggested follow up activities.

Folger series *Shakespeare Set Free*. edited by Peggy O'Brien. This is a series of scripts plus teachers' guides.

Front, Sheila. *Never Say Macbeth*. New York, New York: Doubleday, 1990. FICTION. A boy who wants to be an actor is hired as an apprentice at the Globe Theatre by a famous actor-manager. Jem forgets the superstition about never saying the name "Macbeth" in a theatre, and a chain of humorous events follow.

Garfield, Leon. *Shakespeare: The Animated Tales: Macbeth*. NY, NY: Alfred A. Knopf
Note: This animated tale is based on the televised HBO animated series with introductions by Robin Williams.

"Kids Discover Shakespeare." New York, New York: Kids Discover Magazine, 2000. A user-friendly overview of Shakespeare's times, plays, themes, vocabulary, etc.

Koscielniak, Bruce. *Hear. Hear. Mr. Shakespeare*. Boston, Massachusetts: Houghton Mifflin, 1998. A humorous story that incorporates quotes from Shakespeare as a troupe proceeds to London.

Lamb, Charles and Mary. *Tales From Shakespeare*. Avenel, New Jersey: Children's Classics (Random House), 1986. Shakespeare's plays told in story format.

Morley, Jacqueline. *A Shakespearean Theater*. McGraw-Hill Children's Publishing, 2003. Inside story of the Globe Theatre and the actors.

Mulherin, Jennifer. *Shakespeare for Everyone. Macbeth*. Morristown, New Jersey: Silver Burdett Press, 1988. An easy to read overview of the themes and characters, as well as a scene by scene synopsis of the plot. Also provides information about Shakespeare's times.

No Fear Shakespeare, Macbeth. SPARKNOTES, Spark Publishing, New York, New York, 2003. "The play, plus a translation anyone can understand!"

Rathgen, Elody and Pauline Scanlan. *Getting to Know Shakespeare*. Westminister, CA: Teacher Created Materials, 2003. This resource for teachers includes a variety of plays with activities that relate to themes such as the supernatural and moral dilemmas.

Ross, Stewart. *Shakespeare and Macbeth. The Story Behind The Play*. New York, New York: Viking Press, 1994. Includes excellent background information on Shakespeare's theatre as well as the play.

Shakespeare, William. *The Children's Macbeth*. Santa Barbara, CA: Bellerophon Books, 1996. Large print adaptation of the play.

Simply Shakespeare, Barron's Educational Series, Inc. Hauppauge, New York, 2002. The text of *Macbeth* with a modern line-by-line translation. The text is on one side of each page, and a user-friendly interpretation is on the other side of the page. Also includes an introduction to the play, characters and themes, and role-playing and discussion questions at the end of each scene.

Williams, Marcia. *Tales from Shakespeare*. Cambridge, Massachusetts: Candlewick Press, 1998. Seven plays including *Macbeth* told as a story in cartoon style.

Some websites:

www.Artsedge.kennedy-center.org
(includes lesson plans)

www.folger.edu

NOTES

CD TRACK LIST

1. Boop Boop Pattern
2. Slides and Dynamics
3. Syncopation
4. Scat Phrases
5. Scat Phrases Connected
6. Scat Phrases – Echo
7. The Animals' Gifts
8. Vowel-centric Scat Phrases with Echo
9. Gifts from Gods and Goddesses
10. Pandora's Box: Minor
11. Pandora's Box: Major
12. Pandora's Box Is Opened
13. Pandora's Box: Hope
14. Things Could Be Worse Blues
15. Things Could Be Worse Blues (Blues Accompaniment)

16. Surprise Me!
17. Debka Hora
18. Debka Hora: Moods
19. Debka Hora: Obstacles
20. Hinei Ma Tov ("la")
23. Hinei Ma Tov (Hebrew lyrics)
22. Let's Work It Out – Pop Style
23. Let's Work It Out – Klezmer Style
24. Shalom, My Friends
25. Hinei Ma Tov (with Story Lyrics)
26. Lo Yisa Goy
27. It Could Always Be Worse!
28. How Weird Are These Sisters?
29. Spooky Forest Wind Song
30. Black Spirits